In a Man's World

In a Man's World

Faculty Wives and Daughters at Phillips Exeter Academy 1781–1981

By
Connie Brown

iUniverse, Inc.
New York Lincoln Shanghai

In a Man's World
Faculty Wives and Daughters at Phillips Exeter Academy 1781–1981

iUniverse, Inc.

For information address:
iUniverse
2021 Pine Lake Road, Suite 100
Lincoln, NE 68512
www.iuniverse.com

ISBN: 0-595-28316-0 (Pbk)
ISBN: 0-595-74878-3 (Cloth)

Printed in the United States of America

Credits

Excerpts from *The Garland of Phillipa* by Rosemary Coffin reprinted by permission of Publishing Works, Exeter, New Hampshire © 2001.

Poems by Lilja Rogers reprinted by permission from *More Laughter Than Tears*, The Golden Quill Press, Francestown, New Hampshire©1984.

Excerpts from Fiske and Cilley Diaries used by permission of Judith Fiske Gross.

Excerpts from Peg Aaronian's Meditation used by permission of Peg Aaronian.

Photographs

Photographs of the Exeter Players used by permission of the Exeter Historical Society.

Photographs of Founder's Day recipients:

Katharyn Saltonstall, courtesy of Tinker and Kathy Saltonstall
Helen Potter Stuckey, courtesy of Madeline Stuckey
Jean Kurtz, courtesy of Jean Kurtz Smeeth
Rosemary Honor Coffin, courtesy of Rosemary Coffin
Shirley Brownell, courtesy of David Oxton Photography
Barbara James, courtesy of Barbara James

The Exonian and *The Grapevine*

Exonian articles and *Grapevine* masthead and resources courtesy of the Academy Archives

Cover

Emily Perry's Birthday Party 1927
courtesy of Judith Fiske Gross

"Goodness without knowledge is weak and feeble,
yet knowledge without goodness is dangerous.
Both united form the noblest character and
lay the surest foundation of usefulness to mankind."
John Phillips, Founder.

Dedication

To all who live and work at boarding schools
and who make goodness a full partner with knowledge.

Author's Note

When I began interviewing faculty wives and their daughters at Phillips Exeter Academy, my intention was to gather their life stories and place them in the Academy Archives. As the work progressed, many of the women I interviewed expressed interest in hearing the stories of others. I decided to compile their stories and make them available in the following book. Some of the stories tell of good times, and some of more difficult times. In both cases, one thing is certain—life at Phillips Exeter Academy was always interesting.

Acknowledgements

Thank you to:

The women who shared their experiences as faculty wives and daughters at Phillips Exeter Academy. Their insights into the uniqueness of boarding school life are invaluable.

Barbara Eggers for her original work in 1987.

Jackie Thomas for her encouragement not only of Barbara's work, but of this work.

Ed Desrochers for his encouragement and gracious response to my constant need for information.

Ty Tingley for his encouragement and support.

Elizabeth Rhoades Aykroyd, Marilyn Easton, Lois Gutmann, and Libby Bickel who assisted this effort to completion.

Jane Leonard for photographs from her private collection.

Judith Fiske Gross and Nancy Bissell Goldcamp for their assistance, help in locating daughters, and photographs from their archives and stories.

Judith Dufour of the Exeter Cemetery Association for her help in locating the Phillips plot.

Margie Wachtel for her editing expertise.

My husband, Dick, and son, Dan, for their technical support, editorial advice, patience, and encouragement.

Table of Contents

List of Illustrations

Introduction

What must it have been like for the women who came to live at a school where all the teachers were men and all the student were boys? From the beginning, women faced new experiences in their day-to-day lives as they embraced Phillips Exeter Academy, a secondary boarding school in New England—their new home.

Little has been written about these faculty wives and their daughters. The most expansive work on this topic was done in 1987 by Barbara Eggers, a history teacher at the school. She received a grant from the school to interview the wives of faculty members and women staff members for an oral history.[1] The comments and observations of these women about their lives at the school inspired me to expand on Ms. Eggers' history, including more women and extending the time frame into the first years of coeducation.

I sent questionnaires not only to wives of Emerti but also to their daughters, asking them about their lives at the school and requesting any stories they wanted to share. Of the 164 wives and daughters contacted, 94 responded. I also included interviews and questionnaires from Barbara's original project and information from a panel discussion held in 1977 involving Ellen Scott, Helen Stuckey, Harriette Easton, and Sue Wilson. In addition, sons and brothers who heard of the study added their insights.

Women were important to the school from its inception. Sarah and Elizabeth, John Phillips' wives, contributed financially to the founding of the school though only Elizabeth lived to know the first classes of students at the Academy. The landladies of the boarding houses in

---

1 Ms. Eggers' report is reprinted in the Appendix.

which the students lived served as surrogate mothers. The alumni tell stories about the varying degrees of comfort and comforting they experienced at the hands of these women.

When dormitory quarters expanded to include faculty families, women became an integral part of the all-male school, one made up of male faculty and male students. The first women to live in these dormitories did not always have an easy time of it. Some of these male faculty had difficulty accepting the female and family presence on campus.

Boarding school life is a world unto itself. Most families live in dormitories on campus, eat in the dining hall with the students and other faculty, and act as surrogate parents often inviting students into their homes. They are surrounded by the institution on all sides, unlike non-boarding situations where the families live separated from the work place.

From the Academy's first classes in 1783 until coeducation was instituted in the fall of 1970, only men were hired to teach, and their wives came with them. Wives who were older or who felt more mature and experienced, stepped into the role of faculty wife with relative ease. The same is true of wives who had previous experience in boarding schools as students or wives. Some wives who were very young, inexperienced, or nervous about what lay ahead took longer to decide if "faculty wife" was a role they could fill. Some who were uncomfortable with this role chafed and questioned the expectations the school presented. In the broad picture most wives embraced the private school life, got to know the students and welcomed them into their family life.

The faculty daughters who lived on campus before the school became coed in 1970 commented on what it was like to grow up in an all-male environment. Early childhood was great fun, but the teenage years on an all-male campus had its pros and cons. After coeducation, life for young faculty daughters became easier, generally speaking, but new challenges arose as these girls became teens and entered the Academy as students. Many daughters appreciated the opportunity to think about their years on campus and its effect on their present lives.

The names of the wives in the text are followed by the dates they arrived at the school. The dates after the daughters' name refer to the year they graduated from high school.

The records of this research will be housed in the Academy Archives. If you have stories, accounts or pictures that you think should be included, please send them to the Archives.

Everyone who responded to the questionnaire and who was interviewed was not quoted in the text. But, be assured, your responses are in the archival material and are valued as another contribution to understanding boarding school life as seen outside the classroom.

It has been my privilege to get to know women of all generations and be entrusted with their honest and considered thoughts about their lives at the Academy. The memories and stories recorded here belong to the wives and daughters. Any errors are mine.

Connie Brown Spring 2003

PART I

HISTORY

Chapter 1

Sarah and Elizabeth

In 1741, John Phillips, a native of Andover, Massachusetts, came to Exeter, the home of his grandmother Lydia Gilman, to seek his fortune as a teacher in a small classical school for local youth. After living in Exeter for two years, he decided to become a citizen, paying a tax of four shillings, two pence, a small tax for a very modest income in 1743. He would one day pay a much higher tax when he became the wealthiest citizen of the town, though his wealth would not come from teaching.

John's cousin, Nathaniel Gilman, was a prominent merchant who, at his death in 1741, left a business and estate worth some seventy-five thousand pounds, a considerable fortune at the time. When Nathaniel died, his widow, Sarah, needed help with the accounts and invited John to board at her home while he assisted her in the bookkeeping.

John found this arrangement so much to his liking that two years later, in August of 1743, he and Mrs. Gilman were married. Though she was some eighteen years older than he, the marriage was a happy one as well as a source of profit for John. Women in the 18th century had little control over their finances when they married, so it was important that they marry someone who would be wise in money management. John apparently learned quickly and did well with her inheritance, which upon marriage became his responsibility.

With the change in his fortunes John decided to leave teaching and become a businessman. He bought land on the river side of Water Street, where he built a house, wharf, and landing. Exeter, already 150 years old in 1741, was a small town, clustered around the bank and falls of the Squamscott River. The river afforded the perfect location for a shipping industry. Lumber, which came into town on ox-cart, was sawed and built into ships, which were then exported. He started a business making ship masts and spars for the British Royal Navy, using the King's Pines found in the forests of New England.

3

Sarah and John's home above the business was beautiful, attractively decorated and often the scene of entertaining. Women of that time kept busy visiting neighbors, going to church and lectures, shopping, and going to charity meetings. At home they could paint, play the piano, read, sew, do household chores, and cook. The couple's wealth, made possible by John's wise use of the Gilman funds, afforded them a social position and political contacts in keeping with Sarah's previous position and John's new prosperity. By the time Sarah died in 1765, John, now forty-six, had proven himself an astute businessman.

Two years after Sarah died, John met and courted Elizabeth Dennett Hale, a widow whose husband had been a successful medical practitioner. They married in November of 1767, when they were both forty-eight years old. John and Elizabeth took up housekeeping in the house on Water Street, continuing the business of shipbuilding, and engaging in land speculation and banking.

In 1778, John's nephew, Samuel Phillips, asked for John's help in establishing the Phillips Academy in Andover, Massachusetts. John assisted in the formulation of the constitution of the school, contributed a considerable sum of money, and was made a Trustee for life. John so liked what his nephew had done in Andover that he decided to found a similar school in Exeter.

The constitution for Phillips Exeter Academy (PEA) was based on the one he helped frame for Andover, but with the addition of a religious requirement. His particular interest was in helping scholarship boys of good moral character and intelligence who had an interest in going into the ministry.

Elizabeth's contribution to the Academy at Exeter was profound. By giving up her dower rights in a Deed of Gift she would be dependent on John's stipulation in his will for her support, should he pre-decease her.

John built the first Academy Building on Tan Lane and hired a preceptor and two assistants to teach the first class. His life-long devotion to education became a tangible entity with the establishment of the Phillips Exeter Academy. The money he contributed for the founding of this school was the largest gift of its kind given in America up to 1781.

As it was, when John died in 1795, his will stipulated that Elizabeth was to receive only one thousand silver dollars, the household goods that she had brought with her at their marriage, and fifty dollars' worth of produce annually from the Phillips' farms. The Rev. George Street describes John Phillips' actions in his <u>Historical Sketch of Dr. John Phillips</u>:

> How hardly shall a rich man enter into the kingdom, for he had given it all away with so clean a hand that there was barely enough for the support of his widow for the year or two she survived him. (p15)

Though generous in many ways, John Phillips was excessively frugal when it came to Elizabeth. Not satisfied with the terms of the will, she challenged the arrangement in a letter to the Trustees of Phillips Exeter Academy. On April 21, 1795, the Trustees replied and proposed to allot her fifty pounds, pay her one-hundred pounds annually, give her a cow, allow her the use of her own house and garden and half of the furniture in the house beyond what was her own property. It was understand that the Trustees of Phillips Academy in Andover would supply one-third of the sums mentioned. They gladly added another cow, and Elizabeth was satisfied. She died two years later, in 1797.

Here lyes the Body of Mrs. Sarah Phillips
consort of John Phillips Esq.
Died October 9, 176(?)[5]
in the 65 years of her age.   ·
Elizabeth his second wife died September (?)
1797 Aged 75

(John and his wives were originally buried in the old cemetery on Upper Front Street in Exeter, but in 1865 the Trustees had the remains of the Founder and of his two wives transferred to the new cemetery on Linden Street. (Williams, p18) The original headstone slab for John was moved to the school campus and a new granite engraved slab installed in the cemetery.)

Chapter 2

Classes Begin

Boarding House Landladies

In the late 18th century and early 19th century all students enrolled in PEA were housed with families in town. Though residing in local homes, students were subject to the school rules.

The heads of families...are required to maintain good order...and report to the instructors any instance of disorderly or immoral conduct...Report any student absent from room after ten o'clock in the evening. They shall also report any student who receives visitors on Sunday. No person who refuses or neglects to comply with these rules shall be allowed to receive students into his house. No student is allowed to change his boarding-house without permission.

G.L.Soule, Principal (1838-1873).[2]

Boys were to be in the rooming house, quietly at work, at seven o'clock and in bed by nine o'clock. It probably was not difficult to enforce the lights-out rule because the students had to buy their own candles, which were expensive.

The Academy Archives hold letters and class reunion notes in which students wrote about their boarding house experiences. H. Frank

---

2 Frank H. Cunningham, *Familiar Sketches of the Phillips Exeter Academy*, (James R. Osgood and Co. ©1883), pp 297-8.

Cunningham, in his history of the Academy, *Familiar Sketches of the Phillips Exeter Academy*, includes the following amusing description of one 19th century boarding house landlady and her brood.

Aunt Ringe

In the days of Doctor Abbot, a woman who always went by the name of Aunt Ringe, took students to board. In those days but few boys had fires in their own rooms, and so it was customary for them to study in the living room of the family with whom they boarded. In the house of Aunt Ringe, however, the boys each evening had the dining-room quite to themselves, and on this account it was a favorite boarding-place. A custom of the house was the ringing of a nine-o'clock bell; this was the signal for the boys to fold their books, and like the Arabs, to "silently steal away." They seldom rumbled, or begged to be allowed to sit up later, but, one night after the bell had been rung, they all remained and studied with a zeal which, during the day, would be more commendable than common. Aunt Ringe observed that the young men were not disposed to retire, and so began, after the manner of women, to ask questions. "Boys, didn't you hear that bell?" "O, let us stay a little while longer," said the boys, suddenly disposed to be studious. "Didn't you hear that bell?" was the only response. "Just a few moments more." "Didn't you hear that bell?"

Not even students could stand such a volley of questions, and, worsted in the debate, they retired from the dining-room. Once upstairs, however, they all began to march back and forth, from room to room, in a manner which would have been a model even for the Exeter police force. They took great care not to close the doors *carefully*, and the good lady of the house listened patiently until midnight to the ceaseless tramp of the young Trojans. Then, taking her stand at the foot of the stairs, she called one of the boys down, and, taking him affectionately by the collar, plunged him forthwith out of the front door into the snow. We assure you that he was not long lonesome out in the dark night, for before the bewildered youth could pick himself up and collect his scattered senses, he had company.

Thus, calling all the young patrolmen one by one, she escorted them to the door, and saw them across the threshold. Among the number is said to have been the son of Dr. Gideon Soule. Once out in the stormy night, for the snow was falling fast, these young mischief-makers either walked about in a dazed way till dawn, or else found shelter and solace with some schoolmate.

The next day Aunt Ringe told Dr. Abbot that a few of the boys could return, but some of them never could board with her again. The result was, that she had no boarders the next year, but only for that year, for afterwards her house was ever full. The boys well knew the real kindness of her heart, and, after all, admired her resolution and old-fashioned "New England pluck." In fact, she became quite a heroine.[3]

Not only did town people take in students, but on occasion faculty families would invite students to board with them. The Cilley family was one such family.

A Faculty Family Chronicles Life at the School and How They Become a Boarding House

In his daily diary Bradbury Longfellow Cilley, a teacher of Ancient Languages from 1859 until his death in 1899, sheds light on student activities and how his wife was an integral part of school functions. Amanda and Bradford married in 1864. They started married life in rented rooms in the Bartlett house on Water Street, where Amanda had an opportunity to meet students who boarded there, but for whom she had no responsibility. When they had enough resources to purchase their own home, they looked at Moulton House on Court Street. Because the land across Court Street from Moulton House was a swamp they decided to purchase 15 Elliot Street, farther away and drier, moving there in April of 1871.

---

3 Ibid. p 244+

Amanda's involvement in the town was extensive. She participated in church activities and philanthropic work, and was one of the
chief founders of the Exeter Hospital. Her love of the students and the
school was evident in the numerous ways she contributed to the school
community. It was the custom for the Trustees to examine the Senior
students prior to graduation. After the examinations were completed
there was a bonfire and a procession, followed by a ball that evening,
which Amanda attended as a chaperone. Bradford recorded, "My wife
helps to receive. Day does not end until the next begins."

As a "patroness" for the three big dances held in the Town Hall—
Junior Promenade, Middlers "German" Dance and the June Ball—
Amanda would help the boys plan some of the details, such as what
favors were to be given to the girls.

For a few years Amanda took over the entertaining responsibilities
of the Principal's wife, Mrs. Perkins, who had four small children and
did not have time to fulfill her duties. On another occasion when Mrs.
Wentworth, the interim Principal's wife, was not inclined to act as
hostess for school functions, Amanda gladly entertained the students
and speakers who were invited to the school.

Another diary written by Mabel, Bradbury and Amanda's daughter
born in 1878, affords us a vivid description of their life in the house on
Elliot Street and their venture into being landladies. After Bradbury
died in 1899, Amanda decided to take in a student to help with the
chores.

> Taking care of the furnace, bringing up the coal and taking
> out the ashes, were jobs that we could not cope with, so we
> did what so many did in those days, got an academy boy to
> do it for us. It was not at all uncommon for a boy, by hard
> work, with the aid of a scholarship to put himself through the
> academy. The Academy sent us Frank Dudley.
>
> By Christmas we had learned that he had no place to go for
> vacations, that his room was a makeshift sort of place made
> from the old dining room or kitchen area in the basement of
> Abbot Hall when Alumni Hall was built. It was cold and dis-
> mal, and, as he had made himself so useful, we suggested that
> he have a room here. Many boys worked for their rooms and

this would save him what he was paying for his room and give him what seemed to him a sort of home. As he was here for the next four school years and for the last two years had his meals here, it became the only home he had.

Amanda, wishing to rent a room for revenue, called the Academy office to say that she would like to rent a room to a student.

> Renting rooms to boys was a source of revenue to many in Exeter, but we could never think of it or make it just a matter of money. The boys here were welcome all over the house, were constantly in and out of the living room....They often shared our Sunday breakfasts, the old fashioned kind with steamed brown bread, fish balls and eggs if you wanted them. Frank did come back for his senior year, so for one year we had two students.

Mabel helped with the boarding students at home and worked part-time as librarian at the Academy. Her work brought her into contact with the students and their intellectual needs, as well as keeping her current with the affairs of the school. Even after Amanda died in 1915, Mabel continued to board students.

In 1920 Mabel married Winthrop Edward Fiske, a physics teacher at the school (1899-1938) whose first wife had died. Mabel and Winthrop took up housekeeping in the house on Elliot Street.

Mabel's daughter, Judith, doesn't remember her mother doing much of anything as a faculty wife. Mabel seemed to miss her life as a librarian and her contacts with the students. Judith thought Principal Amen was strict about not wanting the wives involved, and wondered why he felt that way.

Mabel, now a faculty wife, lived in her own home as did other faculty wives at that time. As the school built more dormitories and supplied apartments for faculty, wives found themselves living among the students, and more deeply involved in the life of the school.

The School Grows

The school enrollment increased so much in the late 1800's and early 1900's that there were not enough families in town willing to take in all the students. The school, seeing that there would be a need to supplement the boarding house, decided to create a dormitory in the printing establishment of the Messrs. Williams on Spring Street. The result was so satisfactory that in 1852 the Trustees voted to erect a more suitable and "capacious" building on academy grounds. Abbot Hall was completed and ready for occupancy in 1855. Managed by a matron, it housed students and two teaching assistants, but had no faculty apartments.

When Mr. Francis Ball (1899-1910), a faculty member, was assigned to a room in Abbot Hall, there was no accommodation for his wife. The school made arrangements for her to stay at the Cilleys', while he remained in Abbot Hall. Not finding this a particularly satisfying arrangement, Mr. Ball asked to have meals with the Cilleys as the food there was better than at Abbot Hall and it seemed a "sensible thing to do." The Balls kept this arrangement with the Cilleys through much of that winter before they took up "housekeeping" for themselves.

Dr. Amen, Principal from 1895 to 1913, urged the school to build dormitories and buy houses to accommodate all students, removing the necessity for the students to board with local families. These dormitories and houses also would furnish apartments for the instructors and their families.

A description of Dunbar Hall, built in 1908 for the young 'juniors' or freshmen, showed an intent to have a positive presence of women on campus. Matrons and the faculty wives represented the "refining influence of women" emphasized in this article reprinted in the Exeter Bulletin of 1913.

It is for just such boys [thirteen years old] that Dunbar, with its resident instructors and their families, its quiet, simple home life, its free and intimate companionship with these instructors, was built and equipped....The dining hall is a huge family room; at different tables sit instructors and their families; the refining influence of women is always present. To add to the life in Dunbar, a reading room with papers, periodicals, and many well chosen books, and a game room with a piano are provided. Any evening a group of boys may be seen seated with the matron about the great table in the reading room—a part of the quiet and order of the hall....Not the least of the experiences which the old Dunbar boy remembers with gratitude is the ceaseless attention given to his wants by the loyal and tireless matron.

Life At Phillips, Exeter Bulletin 1913

As the women and children began moving onto the campus into school dormitories, the all-male atmosphere changed. The presence of faculty families in the life of the school was an enormous change that affected the old guard and newcomers alike. Both had to make accommodations and adjustments to their expectations, and this was not an easy task for any of them.

PART II

WIVES

Chapter 3

Woman on the Hall

Many women who came to the Phillips Exeter Academy as wives of faculty in the early 20th century found themselves in a dormitory with the luxury of no rent and all meals provided. Their husbands were responsible for anywhere from sixteen to forty adolescents in their dormitory, coaching a sport each afternoon, and teaching. Privacy was scarce, but on the other hand there was the richness of having the whole campus, safe and well maintained, for their families to enjoy.

Some of the wives did not know what to expect from an all male-boarding school in a small New England town. They felt immature, naive, and unprepared for the challenges posed by sharing their home with adolescent males. Doris Woodbury Leighton was such a wife.

Doris and Harry Leighton had been married one month when they began their life together at Exeter in 1934. They lived in Anderson House, which was leased by the Academy to house one faculty family and fourteen students. The students lived on the second and third floors, where there was one bath tub, two hand basins and one toilet for all of them. The faculty apartment, besides the usual rooms, had an unusual feature: behind and attached to the house was a stable and a black walnut outhouse with three seats: a father-sized, a mother-sized and a child-sized.

Doris' story as she wrote it:

We lived the first four years in a very makeshift dormitory infested by rats and a nosy neighbor who peeked in our bedroom window at night when she watered her dog.

One of our student boys had epileptic fits and once landed against a hot radiator. He had to be cautiously removed.

17

Because I was very young and considered not unattractive I was upset by a critical, unkind letter from some student anonymously my first year. George Major and the Dean tried to trace it quietly without success.

I looked so young that I had a hard time convincing people I was a faculty wife. A student's mother said to me, "You're just a girlie!" And the second Mrs. Perry said, "I thought you were a faculty daughter." No telling what the students thought!

Patty Heath arrived at Exeter in 1947, a young twenty-five. There were no telephones in the dormitory; all calls to the students came through the faculty member's telephone. With Jack out at class, on the playing fields or at meetings, it fell to Patty to answer the calls sometimes requiring her to get out of the bathtub. And the phone rang enough to make it an issue.

The surprise for Helen Clark, who came in 1938 soon after college, was the almost weekly teas, hat and gloves required, which were almost harder to take than the routine of dorm life. For Dot Dunbar, who arrived in 1954 from a small boarding school, the size of the campus and the large number of students and faculty at Exeter were the challenge. As a new wife she was visited in their third floor apartment by the wife of the Dean, who left her calling card, and afternoon teas with white gloves and hats were still being held.

Wives who had lived at boarding schools or had attended them knew what to expect, and most looked forward to the new assignment. Still, there were surprises. At her previous school one wife had a lovely first-floor apartment with a private entrance. When she arrived at Exeter in the 1950's the biggest surprise was that their second-floor Webster Hall apartment had only one door and it opened onto the hall of eighteen students.

Andrea Deardorff (1962) had grown up in a family business and found boarding school life and its demands on her to be surprisingly similar. Carol Hamblet (1979) had been at Governor Dummer before coming to Exeter. For Carol, the dormitory supervision at Exeter was less than had been expected of them at Governor Dummer. Corinna Hammond (1973) expresses her ease with the move to Exeter by stating:

"I was a 'fac brat' at a Harvard house in Cambridge for all my child-hood. I was institutionalized already."

Of the women who arrived on campus under the age of twenty-six, one-third were apprehensive. Of the women twenty-six years old or older, all the women but one faced their new life with ease. It is not surprising that those who had past experience with boarding school life adjusted more easily than those who had none.

(from left to right) Deurie and Dick Rickard, Jane Munro, Gene Finch, Jane and Edith Leonard, Rhoda Clarkson, Mary Rickard, Davis Finch and Lucy Richardson at the Finches' in the 1980's.

(Photo courtesy of Jane Leonard)

Chapter 4

1 BR, No Kitchen, RiverView

One of the biggest challenges for any boarding school is to provide attractive housing for the faculty families. Dormitory assignments were made based on the size of the faculty family and on the need for a balance between experienced and inexperienced faculty. Bachelor apartments frequently were all that were available for new faculty, and the conditions of these apartments could make dormitory living either satisfying or frustrating.

Helen Stuckey started out in 1917 in Peabody Hall where there were fireplaces for which the school supplied the wood. The heat was turned off at noon and turned on again at 5PM, so the fireplaces were most welcome.

In 1925 she and her husband, Howard, moved to Gilman House, a dorm for sixteen students. After being there for a few years, they were asked to leave. It was felt that Dean Wells Kerr wanted his friends, who were square dancers, to live there and use the large living room for dancing. Because the school put steel girders under the living room floor to make it safe for the dancing indicated there may have been some truth to the story.

It was around this time that Dr. Perry made friends with a remarkable man, Mr. Edward Harkness. Mr. Harkness gave monetary gifts to the school three times before challenging Dr. Perry to come up with a new idea for education, an idea that would revolutionize the classroom. In 1930 the idea came into being: The Harkness Table. Each teacher would have twelve students around this oval table, and in the dormitory, only twelve advisees. This would mean hiring twenty-five new teachers and building four new dorms with their own dining halls. Between 1930 and 1935 the faculty went from forty-six members to eighty, the enrollment reached 700 students and all students were housed by the school in seventeen dorms and houses. The newer dorms featured faculty apartments with kitchens and two and three bedrooms, and a few apartments had private entrances. The faculty that had been at the school were able to move into nicer apartments and leave the smaller ones for the new faculty and families coming in under the Harkness plan.

As more faculty were hired, faculty couples began to move into the old bachelor apartments. Few of these apartments had laundries. Moreover the kitchens were often minimal because the bachelors ate most of their meals in the dining hall. Private entrances to the faculty apartments were scarce.

In the 1930's, the school did the flat linens in the school laundry. Otherwise, laundry was done in the bathtub. When washing machines were provided by the school or purchased by the faculty, they were installed in the basement, and the wet laundry was hung up in the dormitory steam room to dry. Rarely was laundry hung outside. One apartment had a patio where clothes might be hung outside, but certainly no feminine underclothes.

In 1935 George Bennett, who had been at the school for a few years, married Violette. The newlyweds were assigned the second-floor apartment in Dunbar Hall. The apartment consisted of several former student rooms separated from the rest of the student rooms by a door across the hallway. Though it was nice not to have to cook, it was a shock to Violette to find that her apartment had one bedroom, one living room, and a bathroom, but *no* kitchen. Eventually a kitchen was added by taking the dressing room away from the main apartment, and installing a sink and refrigerator in the small space. (It remained this way until Dunbar Hall was renovated in 1971.)

> Mr. Richardson and wife Kitty, catching several other boys and myself skinny dipping in the Exeter River...
> (Class of 1930 50th Reunion)

Kitty Richardson and her husband, George Lynde Richardson, had lived in Dunbar Hall from 1919 until 1934 when George died quite suddenly. Dr. Perry honored Kitty's worth to the dormitory and to the preps by keeping her on in the dormitory, where she served tea to the students in the afternoons much like the matrons in earlier years.

When Helen Clark came to the campus in June 1938 the only living quarters available were her husband Bill's bachelor rooms on the top floor of Dunbar Hall. Bill told Dr. Perry he didn't want to bring his new bride up there to start married life with a bathroom and kitchen combined in one small room, and a study and living room combined in another small room. He would rent outside until something opened up. Their bank account was very small, and Helen thought Bill very brave when he told her what he had done. When in 1941 an apartment came available in Soule Hall, they took it. Three years later they moved to a larger apartment in Abbot Hall.

In 1944 with two children we moved into Abbot Hall. Having pre-school children in those days meant restricting their activities and "noise" in the areas near the classrooms. We would bundle them off to the playing fields. The suggestion of putting a sand box behind Abbot was turned down for several years. With no dryers in existence the diapers were hung to dry in the basement steam room, never outside. Help was scarce, but girls from the Robinson Female Seminary, the girls' public high school, would come after school to baby-sit through the dinner hour if a faculty wife wanted to join her husband at dinner. When children became eight years old they were allowed to join us in dining hall.

As far as family living conditions went, the ideal place was Gilman House, our third dormitory, which housed fifteen students. There was plenty of room for four children. Bill's study was separate and accessible. With the kitchen just off the back door and entrance to the boy's rooms, it was easy for a boy to drop in when he needed something or, in the case of homesickness, just to be in a home with children roaming around.

(from left to right) Lucy Weeks with Beth and Lu, Sally Bissell with Nancy and Jack, Ellen Kesler with Jim and Walter. (Photo courtesy of Nancy Bissell Goldcamp)

LaRu Lynch (1939) lived in a second-floor apartment with a door that opened onto the hall of student rooms. She had to carry laundry and their eighteen-month old down two flights to the basement and through the boys' smoking room to do laundry and then up again. In addition, after the students left, when the school turned off the boiler for two weeks of maintenance each June, the faculty had to heat water in big pots on the stove to do laundry.

When Mary and Len Stevens arrived on campus in 1942 they were to be housed on the fourth floor of Merrill Hall in an apartment that had no kitchen and no study. Peter Lloyd, department chairman, objected to the administration, and the Stevens were reassigned to Dunbar. There was still no kitchen, and the bathtub doubled as the kitchen sink, but it was on the second floor rather than the fourth.

During the war years, the Stuckeys were asked to move to the first floor apartment of Amen Hall, an apartment that was long and narrow and had no room for their grown sons should they came to visit. In addition, the students were roller skating up and down the corridors. Not happy with this assignment, Helen took it upon herself to negotiate with Dr. Perry, and he agreed to move them to KEP House for the remainder of their tenure. Because they had no students in KEP the Stuckeys were not allowed to eat in the dining hall. It was wartime, food was rationed, the salaries were low, and it was hard to manage. But manage they did.

The fourth-floor apartment in Merrill Hall, the apartment Mary and Len Stevens did not take in 1942, still had no laundry when Connie and Dick Brown (1962) arrived twenty years later. In fact, there were no machines in the building for that apartment, so Connie went to a Laundromat out on Portsmouth Avenue.

By this time there was a Pullman kitchen in the hallway. There was no counter space or a place to sit down and eat. When counter space was needed, a card table was set up in the hallway. Then, in order to get from one end of the apartment to the other, it was necessary to crawl under the table or to leave the apartment by one door leading onto the student corridor, and then re-enter by another door at the other end of the apartment.

Another dormitory that had a difficult laundry arrangement was Dunbar Hall. Because the Dunbar second-floor apartment had no private entrance, the laundry room was reached by going through the dorm, through the main entrance lobby, into the basement laundry

> Living in Hoyt Hall with Percy Rogers (nice guy) as dorm head. Betting on sex of child to be born to Mrs. Rogers.
> Class of 1930 50th Reunion notes

room. The Dunbar main apartment began on the first floor and included rooms on the second and third floors. This meant gathering the laundry from the second and third floors, going through the common room and main entrance lobby and down to the basement.

Privacy, or rather the lack of it, was often a cause for concern. Many apartments had no private entrance. The families and their guests had to come and go through the student halls. Exeter was not the only school with this issue. Before coming to Exeter, Susan and Phil Wilson worked at Belmont Hill School, where they lived in a private house with eight boys who used the stairway of the Wilson's home to gain access to their rooms on the top floor. By the time the Wilsons came to Exeter in 1942, their three daughters and one son were quite used to dormitory life.

Another example of the lack of privacy could be seen at One Abbot Place, a large clapboard house. Originally the home of the Principal, it became a dormitory when Principal Saltonstall moved to Pine Street in 1946. When Len and Mary Stevens lived in the downstairs apartment, Betty and Dick Brinckerhoff moved into the top floor apartment. The Brinckerhoffs reached their apartment by way of the main staircase, right through the Stevens' apartment. Later, when students were assigned to the top floors, the students also used the staircase to reach their rooms.

Wives found ways to cope with these difficulties, but it was not always easy. Further examples of these inconveniences crop up in the stories that the women relate in other chapters. It was some time before renovations included laundries in a majority of the apartments, real kitchens in the bachelor apartments and private entrances to the faculty apartments.

Chapter 5

Sir, May I Borrow the Key?

Teachers are like that

We're moving to our country home
A half mile from the sea.
We asked to leave our prep school dorm
So that we might be free—
Not of the noise but of the boys'
"Sir, may I borrow your key?"

Quite often people say to us,
"But all your meals were free,
your rent, your heat, hot water, and electricity."
We answer clear, "No more we hear
'Sir, may I borrow your key?'
"But don't you find it lonely there—
just meadows, sky, and sea?
And what about those winter storms
That sweep across the lea!"
This time we shout, to quell all doubt,
"NO BOY ASKS FOR A KEY!"

And yet I know when dorm life's done,
Soon now for Perce and me,
We'll think it would be sweet to hear
"Sir, may I borrow your key?"
                    Lilja Rogers

Keys and Out-of-Towns

The administration of the dormitory rules was not the official responsibility of the faculty wife. Depending on how she and her husband felt about her signing weekend slips, checking boys in at curfew, or loaning the master key to a student who locked himself out of his room, the faculty wife might help or she might not.

When Helen Stuckey was in the dorm in the early 1920's, she was quite willing to participate in dorm management, which she did with Howard's approval. She checked the boys in when Howard was assigned to Senate (Study Hall). Helen became concerned about what a bachelor dorm master would do if there were no one to do duty for him if he had to be away from the dorm. She approached the Secretary to the Faculty, who talked it over with the Principal, Dr. Perry, and it was decided that scholarship boys could be paid to check the boys in when the faculty member was not there. According to Helen this was the beginning of the proctor system where students were elected by their dorm mates to do check-ins, be there as a friend, and act as liaison with the faculty.

When the Lynches lived on the first floor of Webster they had a thousand knocks at the door, mostly from boys who had locked themselves out of their rooms. LaRu remembers Ranny's thoughts on giving out the key:

> Ranny thought that it was a good thing for them to stay locked out a bit once in a while. Sometimes he would take the key with him so that I couldn't let them in. I think that Ranny felt that so many of the boys had been brought up by their mothers and grandmothers and their first teachers were women that now here they were in a boy's school and they should learn to get along in a man's world. I didn't much like my position but I had to do it.

> One of the great things about Exeter is that you can do what feels is right for you. There is a lot of space for individuality, which I think goes right through into the teaching and the athletic field.

Ranny could be separate from the family because you had to open the apartment door and go down the hall to get to his study. There were other people who felt differently. When another faculty member went to check the boys in, he took his little son by the hand and they went around together.

Andrea Deardorff took an active role right from the beginning. Based on her experience teaching high school before she arrived in 1962, she made a point of getting to know the students. She anticipated the arrival of the new students by studying the student folders so that she knew the faces and names of the boys. She felt that by letting them know she was aware of each and every boy that they would feel more comfortable with her personally.

Carole Rindfleisch (1968) never went into the boys' dorm, but on the other hand, Frances Ekstrom (1969) lived in a one-faculty dorm and helped her husband, Jim, by signing weekend permissions slips, giving out keys, etc. since there was no one else to do it. Joyce Morgan (1969) also was active in the dorm. "I did not give out the dorm key, I took it to the room. I signed permission slips with *my* name so that there would be no confusion."

Walter Pierce encouraged Nancy (1971) to help in dorm since she was summer school dorm faculty and used to doing duty. Nancy "signed slips and gave out the master key. Since I was staying home with our babies, I felt I could support Walt, especially in the dorm, by taking various boys under our wing. Some of them were so young and away from home and really needed the TLC of a family."

Carol Hamblet (1979) was always willing to help Chuck in his job although she doesn't remember ever feeling that she needed to *do* his job. "My helping him gave us more personal time together. I was available to give out the master key, though I did not sign permission slips. I did not feel I should be responsible for a signature since I had no official role. I did check students in until Chuck arrived home, usually from an away basketball game."

In contrast, Carole Tucker (1980) did little in the dormitory. "George was clear about the 'rules' back in our days in the dorm. I did, however, have a lot of students who assumed it was okay to check in with me or to leave messages. Sometimes when George was 'Dean on duty'

I felt the need to escape to avoid acting as a legal substitute for check-in or problems."

In May 1986 Tootie Cole (1947) wrote the following article about dormitory life for the Academy's Committee to Enhance the Status of Women (CESW) Newsletter, in which she describes her goal and her formula for success.

On Residential Life

During the 1950s and 60s I spent seventeen years living in a dormitory as a faculty spouse. I enjoyed those years sharing in the life of the dormitory. Raised in dorms myself, I was aware of the benefits of living on campus and had previous experience in the process of juggling family privacy with dormitory commitments.

My aim was to help improve the dorm atmosphere and to do as much as possible to save time for Don so he would have time for us. I took in weekend slips for signatures, supervised the use of the master key if it was used on a floor I could see from one of my doors, took down 'phone messages (before the proliferation of 'phones in the department rooms and student area) and made my presence known during unusual disturbances. We gave birthday parties and had students in to watch special events on TV. Don was on the football field each September as students arrived on campus, so I met all our advisees and their parents, explaining procedures, memorizing those who had unusual family situations, and noting concerns about classes, roommates and medical quirks.

In those years students were more independent then they are now (once their parents left). It was expected that advisers would give pep talks on improving grades at marking periods. We now joke about how Don would give out the grades and make at times heated comments and suggestions to students for improvement while, as the often shaking boys left the apartment, I would commend them for their achievements while handing out brownies.

There were several considerations I felt were helpful to those who had to share life with us. I used hook and eye latches up high on doors leading out to the dorm to protect us from wandering students and particularly students from wandering Coles. When we lived in Langdell I brought the children in from the quadrangles by five so young piercing voices would not disturb the evening classes. We were particularly sensitive to this since Gramps Wilson and Don taught in the two end rooms on the first floor of Phillips Hall.

We moved out of the dorm after seventeen years when time commitments of the school and family requirements of older children seemed to be clashing. I believe the role I played was important, allowing Don to handle his "triple threat"*duties as well as extra administrative assignments and family responsibilities. In these modern times the spouse who fulfills this function should be given an official and financial identity.
*Teaching, coaching and advising in dormitory

How involved the wife became in assisting her husband in the dorm depended on how much the wife wanted to do, as well as how much the faculty member wanted her to do. From the comments the wives made, it appears that those wives who assisted their husband in the dormitory felt happier about their lives at the school than those who did not help their husbands.

Pizza, Cookies and Lemonade

When the new students and their parents arrived on campus the school expected the wives to preside at receptions for which the school provided the lemonade and cookies. Otherwise, wives were free to entertain as they wished, or not at all. It was obvious the students appreciated home-cooked food, any day of the week and in any form.

For many years the dormitory faculty did not receive funds for the entertaining of the students. Consequently most faculty used their limited dorm funds or private funds to provide the food they themselves wanted to share with the students. The variety of foods offered and styles of presentation illustrate the ingenuity of the wives and their entertaining skills.

The Stuckeys (1917) entertained the boys on Saturday nights as well as the frequent shout into the dorm, "Who wants coffee? Who wants something cold to drink?" Not only the students appeared, but so did Kathy and Bill Saltonstall (1932) who also lived in the dorm.

LaRu Lynch (1939) had two stories about birthdays. The first year they lived in Webster Hall, Ranny had twenty-two advisees, seventeen of them named Michael:

> One Michael came down for his birthday party about 5PM, before dinner, and we always said come after dinner. He just sat in the kitchen and finally I said, "Well, Michael, wouldn't you like to invite some of your friends in?" And he said, "I don't have any friends." So he sat there and munched cake by himself.

> Another Michael was Michael Rockefeller. When it was his turn to come down, he appeared with between fifteen and twenty friends. And I wondered whatever will we do with only this one cake. So, we cut it in very small pieces and everything was okay until suddenly Michael said, "Here come my Mother and my Grandmother. They've just parked the car." In comes Mrs. Nelson Rockefeller and everybody laughed and we had a good time. Unfortunately they didn't bring a cake.

Andrea Deardorff (1962) preferred to be spontaneous—to have the students prepare things themselves and help with clean up. In her experience if they had something to do with their hands they talked more easily. She varied the approach: make your own pizza, put together a banana split, make popcorn, grill hamburgers. A house rule was that the student had to stay in the apartment to eat, not take food back to his room.

Before coeducation graduation weekend posed an unusual challenge in two ways. There were no easily identifiable women's lavatories on campus, so grandmothers, mothers and sisters came to faculty apartments when they needed a bathroom. In addition, there was no provision for lunch for the graduates and their families after the graduation ceremony.

The Deardorffs opened their home to their students' families, and took it upon themselves to provide something to eat. Andrea remembers making sandwiches by spreading out a loaf of bread along the counter, going back with a filling, back again with another filling, like an assembly line. The school eventually stepped in and hosted a lunch under a tent or in the field house for the entire senior class and their families.

Jean and Dave Walker (1963) had an open door to all TV sports events. Another wife had a buffet breakfast for boys and their dates on dance weekends. Dorm meetings were occasions for hospitality for Nancy Pierce, and Halloween a time for fun antics.

Joyce Morgan (1969) recalls that "often the school did not actually ask us to entertain, but left lemonade concentrate and cookies at my door." On her own she made cookies or brownies. On Saturday nights at check-in, Joyce and Brian turned their home into Morgano's Do-It-Yourself Pizza, or the Morganie Creperie, Morganoff's Tearoom, or Morganez' Taco Joint.

Carol Hamblet (1979) made a practice of providing snacks for the students. "While Chuck was on duty in the evening I would often bake cookies and share them with the students. One night while Chuck was in his study giving extra math help I made a batch of cookies and I *burned* them. The house smelled like burnt cookies so I thought I would be funny and fixed a plate of the cookies. I took them in to the boys who were working with Chuck. I certainly got a good laugh when they ate every cookie on the plate—they didn't care that they were burnt!!"

Carol Tucker (1980) put out chocolate Easter eggs and holiday treats at the students' doors, and had the proctors in for dinners. One outstanding meeting is fresh in Carol's mind. "We had a very articulate, bright group of students in Wentworth who were curious about exactly what Trustees did. The three trustees who came to the common room for coffee were astonished at the penetrating questions the students asked."

The wives used a lot of imagination in the variety of ways they tried to make the students feel more at home. Whether it was birthday parties or food for students when the faculty were on duty Saturday night, the wives were generous with their time and expertise.

Chapter 6

Campus Capers

At the Door

A wife never knew what prompted a student to knock on her door until she opened it. Before one of the dances a student came to Patty Heath and asked if she would remove his blackheads for him. "Needless to say, I didn't," she assures us.

Shirley and Bob Brownell (1958) "were sitting in their dormitory apartment living room when a young man walked in the front door. He ascended the stairs to our bedroom level believing he was in the students' part of the dorm. We did not follow him up. A few minutes later he came down, sheepishly, and walked back out. He was nice enough to know 'I've done it now.'"

To the Door

In the 1950's the faculty apartment on the second floor of Webster Hall had its only entrance door at the end of the hall of student rooms. A wife remembers: "I was busy with something requiring concentration when I heard a thumping coming regularly down the hall and bouncing on our door and then retreating. This went on for seven or eight minutes, and it was during study hours. It could only be a lacrosse ball to sustain that momentum. I stood it as long as I could, then went to the door and listened until the ball was almost at the door. Staying out of sight, I opened the door—and closed it after the ball was inside. Peace and quiet again. No one ever came after that ball."

In 1962, one trick was to flip bottle caps down the length of the hall. When the student hall paralleled the hall inside the faculty apartment, the pinging lasted a long time.

Who's calling?

Before the students had pay phones in the basement, all phone calls came through the faculty apartments. Because the faculty wives were at home more than the husbands, the women frequently had the job of going into the dorm to find the students. This was one of the occasions when wives ventured into the dorms. If the student was not in the dorm, it was hard for some parents to understand why the wife could not conjure him up! One mother from California always got the time zone differences backward so when the Seabrookes ' phone rang at 3:00AM they knew who it was.

Van Moutis arrived on campus in 1954, a twenty-six year old bride. The Moutis' first home was a two-room apartment on the 3rd floor of Cilley Hall. One room had been divided in half to form a kitchen with a partition to form the bathroom, and a bedroom. The other room was a combination study and living room with a walk-in clothes closet next to the front door and a telephone next to the closet door.

One evening, Van, in her underwear, was in the closet looking for something to wear when the phone rang. Nick answered it, and went off in search of the student. The student came in and stood at the door of the closet, proceeding to carry on a long conversation. Van, in the closet, was suffocating and nervous that the student would find her there. Finally the student left and Van "asked" Nick how he could do that to her!

Jackie and Dave Thomas (1957) were living in the Wheelwright apartment on the 4th floor. One Sunday morning Jackie was home alone, curled up in bed feeling miserable. A student's mother called and asked Jackie to find her son and bring him to the phone. Jackie said she was too sick to go into the dorm right now. The mother said, "When will you feel better?"

Flu epidemic strikes campus!

The Flu Epidemic of 1918 sent at least 100 boys at a time to bed. When the Infirmary, Hooper House, could not house everyone, the old Gymnasium behind the Academy Building was pressed into service. When that filled up the faculty wives acted as nurses in the dorms.

In the 1950's Dot Dunbar remembers faculty wives being pressed into service as *de facto* nurses, instructed in how to take care of the overflow of students confined to the dorm because the infirmary could not hold all the afflicted. There were three flu epidemics in the history of the school, all of which called upon the wives to minister to students in the dormitory.

TV as New

The Dunbar Common Room was the location of the first TV on campus in a public place. It was a beautiful machine donated by one of the boys, the son of a person who was running early TV. It was locked in a cabinet and Sue Wilson kept the key. The boys could watch only from 7:00 to 8:00 in the evening. If something special was scheduled, it could be opened up with permission.

Inside the Apartment

Rosemary Coffin (1953) found that when she had guests from town coming to dinner, she had to remind them to bring a warm sweater because the heat in the dorm was turned off for the night at ten o'clock.

These Aliens Weren't Students

A Charlotte Manning (1963) story:

> We were living in Merrill Hall. On a summer evening my son Paul, age six, and his pal, John Walker, pitched a tent in the quad and decided to spend the night. Between 8:00 and 10:30 they made innumerable climbs up to our 3rd floor

apartment, getting food, going to the bathroom, etc., etc. Finally I declared that one more appearance and they would spend the rest of the night indoors.

In the morning Paul reported their adventures, including that they had seen a very bright light in the sky-much bigger than an airplane—slowly descending toward the ground. He wanted to get us but remembered my ultimatum.

A few days later, we were at supper with the McIlhenys, listening to their description of a couple's abduction by extra-terrestrials on a highway near Exeter. The story was told in the book, *Incident at Exeter*, and also made into a TV movie. I have always wondered...

Outside the Window

Carole Hamblet (1979) tells of incidents involving their boys' dormi-tory:

It was the middle of the night and we were sound asleep. Our dog, Tori, barked so much that we figured something must be wrong. We discovered a girl climbing down the Webster boys' dorm fire escape.

Surprise—marijuana growing in my garden. It seems that the cigarette butts tossed out the windows the year before had taken root and grown into mature plants. The day the proc-tors returned in September, the plants disappeared.

The day the students arrived on campus, it was all confu-sion. A boy ran into our apartment yelling, "They're stealing our TV!" We rushed out to find the TV sitting in the driveway and the thieves nowhere in sight. Ozzie Bettencourt, a student from Brooklyn, NY, had yelled out the window, "Stop or I'll shoot!" The thieves obviously thought he was serious. As if that was not good enough, another student, seeing the police,

police, came up and asked what was going on. Hearing that
the TV was almost stolen, the student pulled a dollar bill out
of his wallet and said, "That car looked suspicious so I wrote
down the license number." The thieves were picked up later
that day at UNH where they were doing the same thing.

In the Classroom

Hilary Heyl, three years old, showed up in Mr. Gropp's German
class, *naked*. He gave her a paper and pencil to amuse her, then thought
better of it. He walked her to the nearest faculty apartment, and asked,
"Who *is* this?" The faculty wife replied, "Nancy must be frantic!" and
took over.

In the Hospital

Nancy Pierce (1971) had a delightful experience with two students
in her dorm:

> We lived in Cilley and several boys had to stay through the
> Thanksgiving holiday because it was too far to go home. I
> think the break was only one or two days. My pregnancy
> came to a happy ending the night before Thanksgiving when
> Toddy was born. Two 9th graders in our dorm asked Walt if
> they could come to the hospital to help bring her home. Walt
> agreed. They arrived in the nursery while Walt was paying
> the bill and told the nurse they wanted to see their cousin. The
> nurse was just a bit surprised as they were black and in 1971
> there were few black babies in Exeter! They loved describing
> the nurse's expression. When we got home, they checked in
> with us every hour to make sure Toddy was OK!

The Midnight Slam

According to Helen Stuckey, early in the 1920's it was the last night
before the undergraduates left and the campus was vibrating with the

final packing and excitement of departure. At the stoke of midnight the boys slammed the doors of their rooms all at the same time. The faculty, determined to put an end to this foolishness went around afterward and checked to see if there was dust over the door. If none, the door had been slammed and the door came OFF.

The Slam was abandoned and replaced by the "Midnight Scream," harder to document. Just before midnight, the faculty took up positions on the lawn outside the dorms, readied their pencils and clipboards and watched for which windows opened and who leaned out. The faculty were not to be out-foxed by mere adolescents.

In the Kitchen

Pam and Rick Parris (1978) lived in Lamont Dormitory when a student in their girls' dormitory adopted their family and their kitchen and their basement and their living room, and…their hearts. Pam describes how one girl, a four-year student, became a part of their family:

A Sunday afternoon in September was the first visit that I remember. I recognized her as one of the new students in our dorm. I was pleased she had knocked on the door of our apartment. I didn't expect she'd stay five hours.

She came often after that, for short visits and long. She talked. She played with the children. Sometimes she seemed like one of them, vying for a toy or a turn to read. When it was time for dinner, it was hard to get her out the door. Sometimes she had a bowl of pasta with us.

Many evenings, she came to say goodnight to the children. Her face fell if they were already in bed. She smiled with anticipation if they weren't, and she was happiest if she'd arrived just in time for milk and fresh, hot cookies. She ate plenty of them but never wanted the milk. She disliked it, she said. Until the night when we were running low and I told the kids not to drink too much or there'd be none for breakfast. She looked me right in the eye and said slowly, "May I have some, please?" "I thought you didn't like milk," I said. "Tonight I'd REALLY like some." I poured her a half glass, no more or less than I'd given to my own children, with the vague feeling I was being put to a test.

Fall wore on and Halloween was coming. Most of our dorm devised simple costumes with what they had. But I already could guess that no such solution would do for our adopted daughter. After much consideration, she had decided to be a nun. "Where can you get the costume?" I inquired. I should have known. "I'm going to make it myself. Can I use your sewing room?" she chirped. "Sure, but where will you get the fabric?" I asked, getting myself in deeper. The plan grew, and, of course, it involved me. She wanted to dye her bed sheets in a big tin washtub she had bought at a hardware store and would return to get her money back afterward. My kitchen floor was her preferred location. I pictured a black brew sloshing onto the beige linoleum as she stirred the pot like a witch of the season. This time I had to be firm; I told her she could use our patio. But efforts to package this girl's enthusiasm never worked. When Sunday afternoon came, a cold rain poured down, making outdoor dyeing impossible. We compromised on the basement, and for the rest of our time in that apartment, dark stains on the cellar cement reminded me of that October. Each day that week she came to cut, to plan, to fit, to learn to use my elderly sewing machine to construct the enormous garment. She fretted constantly that the color had turned out disappointingly gray, but on Thursday I saw her running out of Phillips Church, flagging me down. "It's OK," she called. "I just found out there ARE nuns who wear gray! *Isn't that WONDERFUL?*" I had to agree it was. On Halloween, the costume made the rounds, probably under-appreciated by the public but much enjoyed by its maker.

The next big project came at the term's end. She had decided to bake a cake for one of her classes and again wanted to use my kitchen. Another girl approached me with the same request; this girl had brought what she needed, baked, cleaned up and left, all in an hour. I knew it would be different with our special friend, and it was. After hearing long explanations for the lack of this and that, I provided her with many ingredients. The measuring and mixing, all done with characteristic exuberance, took over a half-hour. The baking had to be rigorously regulated, the cooling time carefully supervised. The clean-up, since nearly every bowl I owned had been mobilized for the project, was a major operation. Alas, the frosting, for long and well-documented reasons, would have to be done the following day. So there she was, twenty-four hours later, stirring and sifting again. I was called away briefly, and on my return, the mess had expanded further. "You know," she said, licking her fingers, "I think I finally know where EVERYTHING in your kitchen is!!" I managed a smile. "Except," she added, "Do you have any blue food coloring? That's the ONE thing I couldn't find." Her hands and teeth were soon as blue as the icing. A cook like this doesn't create without tasting her way to perfection. When at last the masterpiece was complete, there was, of course, a reason I no longer remember as to why the cake could not be kept in her room. She would need to return the next day to pick it up. Would I be home? Yes, of course.

And so it went. Nothing was ever simple with some people, I told myself. They just needed it not to be. Little by little her story trickled out: an unfortunate childhood. A broken home. A need to recoup lost time, missed experiences.

Four years passed. It was time for our other child to leave. After the graduation lunch in the dorm, her mother took both my hands in hers. We had seen little of this parent in those four years, but somehow she knew. "I don't know why she's like this," she said. "I know what you must have done, and I thank you because I love her very much." I assured her that we did too. We wondered how we would ever say good-bye to this child who had so enlivened the place since her arrival as a prep at only thirteen. But it wasn't a problem. Mom was leaving separately, and her daughter had been promised a ride to the airport in a limousine, hired by the parents of another graduate. It had just glided in, even longer, blacker and more glittering than in the girls' dreams. They squealed and tumbled in, vying to figure out its myriad gadgets and stroke the velvet seats. "Good-bye! Good-bye and thanks! They giggled. The door thudded shut, silencing their voices. Opaque windows cut our view. We sighed in relief. It was over. It would be different now. We would miss her.

Though Pam Parris is not "retired" as of this printing, her narrative is included because it describes the reality of dorm life so vividly and poignantly.

Chapter 7

Dinner and Dancing

In the Dining Hall

The Dining Hall experience was an integral part of residential life. The faculty member was responsible for being at meals the day he was on duty in the dormitory to insure faculty presence at every meal.

Up until the late 1960's, faculty were assigned to a table with other faculty members for each and every meal. Scholarship students wearing white coats served them. Wives could come or not, as they chose. When faculty children had to be at least eight years old in order to have a place at the table, many wives hired baby sitters for the supper hour, allowing the wives to have dinner with their husbands, have time without the children, or join other faculty for coffee and dessert in faculty apartments.

One wife remembers sitting in Dunbar Dining Hall, at her assigned table, feeling quite uncomfortable. Over her head was a painting of a middle-aged woman walking her female dog that was obviously "in heat" and being followed by a pack of male dogs. The picture was still there when the dining hall was closed down in the 1980's.

Before coeducation, "females" were such a rarity on campus that on one occasion when a faculty wife wore a tight-fitting sweater to Webster Dining Hall, the boys actually lined up to get a view. She never did that again, and neither did any of the teenage daughters.

The ever increasing number of students and faculty forced a change in the dining system. Eventually all students and faculty went through the cafeteria-style line and no students served as waiters. Though there were tables set aside for faculty no one was assigned to sit with anyone in particular.

In May of 1969 the age for children to join their parents was reduced to six, and in December 1986, the age restriction was lifted totally, and children could be in the dining hall from birth, though there was opposition to children being at table from faculty who did not want to lose the hour of adult conversation. On the other hand, the new ruling meant that the families could share meal times.

Dining Hall privileges had their pros and cons. Each family had to decide for itself what was most important. Currently all faculty families, living in dorms and off campus as well, are welcome at all meals. Families can eat all together, and faculty who live off-campus can come and keep up with campus news.

On the dance floor

Before coeducation, the three major dances involved the entire school. The girls who were invited as dates tended to be girlfriends from back home or blind dates, imported from a variety of schools. The big dance weekends such as that sponsored by the Southern Club were gala affairs. Live bands, decorations, chaperones, white gloves and "cutting in" were commonplace. Dances were held in the Thompson Gymnasium or in the Assembly Hall, called the Chapel, where the wooden benches could be removed and stacked in the hall, leaving the whole room free for dancing.

Judith Fiske Gross (daughter, 1942), inspired by a photograph of "patronesses," which appeared in the Winter 1996 *Exeter Bulletin*, remembers her first dance, where she was unprepared to be introduced "in such an elegant manner. At a later one, I was introduced by the wrong name, which was quite funny since the ladies knew who I was perfectly well. We all tried hard not to smile too much so as not to embarrass the usher. Even my date politely smiled. Those were very happy times in my life. Looking at the picture I can still smell the mixture of gardenia corsages and the odor of chlorine from the swimming pool at a dance in Thompson Gymnasium."

In the very early days it was an honor for a faculty wife to be asked by the Senior Council to chaperone their dance as a Patroness. Helen Stuckey (1917) remembered it well. "The fashion was to wear a long dress and white gloves. The boys called for you in a carriage from the Livery Station, a house behind the Post Office and Gorham Hall. You were helped into the carriage and escorted to the Gym, which was behind Abbot Hall. As nice as all that may have been, the horses smelled terrible."

Libby Bickel (1936), too, was asked to be a Patroness at the dances, and also, being young and attractive, had to hold off the students. "I was dancing with a student I knew, when another student tapped him on the shoulder to dance with me. He asked if I was Walter's girl. I said, 'No, I'm a faculty wife.' It was flattering for me, but a jolt for the student."

Usually asked to be a patroness, Barbara Little (1939) went to the Southern Club Dance in 1943 as an invited guest of a senior who had no date. Nancy Heyl (1947) was asked to chaperone "endlessly." As a patroness she was not asked to dance until she asked the president of the Southern Club to stop treating the women like chairs or punch cups. Then she was danced off her feet!

The second kind of dance was the less formal dorm dance. On Saturday afternoon, busloads of girls and their chaperones were imported from girls' schools for dinner and a dance in the evening. When the girls arrived after lunch, they were assigned a partner—*by height*.

When Jackie Thomas' husband, David, was head of the Dance Committee, he made arrangements with girls' schools for Saturday dinner and dances both at Exeter and away at the girls' school. Jackie (1957) remembers what it was like to go to the girls' schools:

We left for the school at 4:00 in the afternoon, and got back to Exeter between midnight and 1:00AM. If you were a smoker, the husband of the head mistress had to escort you outside. Patty Heath and I would sit with the women chaperones, then sit through dinner, and the dance.

Back on campus, for the Amen Hall dances, we went into the girls' bathrooms and hauled the girls out of the stalls. During the dances, couples that were dancing too close were admonished with a kick.

The dances, both formal and informal, were the main source of socialization on campus for the boys before coeducation. The interactions between the students and the girls were often stilted and emphasized only the social aspects of relationships. By their grace and example as chaperones, faculty wives exemplified for the students and their dates the social conventions of the day.

80 Effervescent Rogers Hall Girls Fry 'Burgers, Twist with Exonians

by Charles McCormack

Eighty girls from Rogers Hall came to Exeter early Saturday night, and left late, after experiencing "the most completely different dorm dance" in the recent history of the Academy.

The girls arrived at the Music Building around 5:30 and met their dates for the evening. The Exonians attending the dance were from Dunbar, Wheelwright, Abbot Place, Faculty Circle, and Kirtland House.

While the residents of Wheelwright, Faculty Circle, and Kirtland and their dates had dinner in the Wheelwright dining hall, those from Dunbar and Abbot Place gathered informally with their dates in the beautifully-decorated Dunbar common room, and cooked hamburgers over an open fire in the fireplace.

Some of the stalwart girls gladly offered their services in History Instructor and Mrs. Jeffrey R. Fleischmann's kitchen, while a few brave young men flipped hamburgers on a grill in the fireplace. "Three kitchens at R. H., and we can't cook at all there," said Debbie Wood, busy tossing a salad.

The atmosphere in Dunbar, in contrast to Wheelwright, was not strained. The couples mixed freely throughout the preparation and dinner.

The atmosphere at the dance in the Music Building was relaxed. "It was a happy dance," said Ted Drake, who organized the dance almost entirely by himself.

"It was the best dance I've ever been to," commented Judy Greene, vice-president of the Student Council at Rogers Hall. The girls said they were very happy, and were particularly impressed with the dinner in Dunbar and the type of introductions.

The girls repeatedly expressed their preference for Exeter men over Andover boys.

The Exonian December 18, 1962

Chapter 8

On Campus

Faculty wives contributed to the school in ways other than dormitory affiliation. They sought employment or volunteer work on campus within the guidelines the school established at a given time. Barbara Little (1939) thinks she became the first woman teacher when Dick Mayo-Smith came down with the mumps and a substitute was needed for three or four weeks. "I was not paid and didn't think a thing about it. Regarding one homework assignment I recall a boy asking me, 'Do we have to know this?' and when I answered with a firm, 'Yes,' the boy instinctively and politely, respectfully even, said, 'Yes, Sir.'"

Mary Stevens in the 1940's put out the Daily Bulletin for Jim Griswold, worked in the Library and was Assistant to Glen Krause, Director of the Gallery. In the 1950's Betty Caspar applied to Corning Benton, treasurer, for a position. He allowed that some women were hired as typists in the peak seasons. Betty went to work in the Alumni Office, where she stayed for several years. The Exeter Bookstore hired faculty wives Betty Brinckerhoff, Tootie Cole and Ellie Tremallo, who were visible examples of how faculty wives used their expertise.

Margot Trout (1961) had an unfortunate experience as an art teacher:

> I worked off campus teaching art part-time at UNH. Then I was invited to teach in Exeter Summer School which I did successfully for three years. When a position opened up in the art department during the regular session I was told that they needed "new blood." My impression was that faculty wives would not be considered but I'm not sure whether it was a formal or informal policy. I was more qualified than the person they hired and was so angry at this that I wouldn't teach

in the summer school any more. I still get furious whenever I think of it.

In the 1970's Joyce Morgan noticed that, though there was no school policy about wives working off-campus:

> ...it was thought that wives could not join the faculty because it would violate some sort of nepotism rule. (Brothers, fathers, and sons could teach—just not wives.)
>
> It affected me personally, really only because it was profoundly offensive. I taught at Governor Dummer for a year as a substitute, at UNH in the Russian and English departments, and eventually established a grades 7-12 Russian program in the Exeter public school system. I also taught in the PEA Summer School until my husband, Brian, became Director. There was no job for me in the Academy Russian department until so late that I was already firmly ensconced in the Junior and Senior High School Russian program which I had started and was not interested in leaving.

In the regular session the need for dorm supervision by faculty members and by someone who could be present during the day was an on-going topic of discussion. What, if any, official role should the wives have in the dormitory? One way to test the abilities of the women and the feasibility of having them employed in the dormitory was to hire them for Summer School dormitory supervision. Van Moutis, Patty Heath, Carol Rindfleisch and Nancy Pierce were the first faculty wives to be employed in dormitory supervisory positions, proving that women could do the job, and do it well.

When Nancy Pierce (1971) was at the Academy in the 1970's she worked as a dormitory supervisor in the Summer School. She was not allowed to work in the dormitory in the regular session as a dorm supervisor. "It affected Walter and myself personally. If PEA had allowed me to do dorm duty in the regular session, we might have stayed. Walt felt that he could not teach four math classes well, coach two varsity sports and do dorm duty without feeling he could not do it to his standard and the school's expectations."

Jacquelyn Thomas proved to be the exception to the rule. Jackie and her husband, David, arrived in 1957, to a fourth floor Wheelwright apartment which had no kitchen. When the school finally installed a kitchen a year later, the refrigerator was outside the apartment on the stair landing and the hot plate was in the bathroom. "Eventually the hot plate was replaced by the baby. The washer and dryer were five floors down, and we paid for them ourselves. When we moved to Amen, the school asked us to buy another washer and dryer, and we refused. It took another year to get a room for the baby. It was a fight all the way."

Another difficulty for the faculty was the lack of private yards. Jackie and Dave lived in Amen Hall, they put out a sandbox and play equipment for their children, despite tradition.

Jackie was active in the town and at the school, acting in plays for the Exeter Players, and doing make-up for boys in the all-male casts at the school. She served orange juice in the infirmary and entertained parents and Trustees, helped found the Volunteers of the Exeter Hospital and served on their Board, held a position in League of Women Voters, and served as a Trustee and treasurer of the Exeter Day School.

One rule for which Jackie was the exception was that few wives did not work outside the home in the 1950's. However, before her first child was born, Jackie did work part-time, then full-time, in a local bank. One evening at the dining hall dinner table Jackie's employment was mentioned. There was dead silence. When an older faculty wife voiced her disapproval a male faculty member thought a moment and then said, "I think that might be all right."

The Academy did not hire wives for full-time positions at the school until well into the 1970's. When her family was grown, and Jackie returned to work in 1971, it took a decision of the Trustees for Jackie to be hired by the school full-time in the library. She became the only faculty wife with faculty status at the time she became Head Librarian in 1975.

Joyce Morgan and Sharon Hamilton also experienced censure from faculty men about working though several years apart. Joyce reports the following conversation and results:

Newly retired to motherhood from their college teaching, and newly arrived at PEA in the 1960's, they both attended a cocktail party, though seven years apart. The conversations proceeded in similar fashion despite the time difference, as related by Joyce:

> An older, male faculty person, whom I had never met, after the usual preliminaries said, "And what did you used to do, dear?
>
> I replied, "I used to teach."
>
> He said, "How nice, and what grade was that, dear?"
>
> My reply: "Well, it was college, actually."
>
> The older faulty person turned on his heels and abruptly walked away.
>
> Neither Sharon nor I could quite forget the weirdness. It seemed so 19th century and unlike anything either of us had ever experienced.

The Exonian, the school weekly newspaper recorded some of the activities and thoughts of the wives in the following articles. The Debating Society gave the wives the opportunity to show their lighter side, defending their presence on campus on two occasions at the Daniel Webster Debating Room in June 1961 and December 1962. Other articles outline what interested the wives in the 1960's.

McIntosh Sings, Mrs. Vernet Enchanting; Faculty Wives Show Boys Hate Mothers

by Nicholas Deane

At left, affirmative speaker Thomas Bilodeau makes a point. Right: Mrs. Vernet speaks for the victorious negative team.

Three faculty wives, debating the negative side of the topic, *Resolved:* "A Mother Is a Boy's Best Friend," won a debate against Thomas Bilodeau, Ted Drake, and DeCourcy McIntosh. The well-attended debate was held Wednesday evening in the Daniel Webster Debating Room.

The high point of the debate was the rebuttals. Mrs. André R. Vernet won the debate for her team in a short, wistful, dictionary-supported rebuttal. She pointed out that a friend, according to the dictionary, is someone outside of the family. A well-calculated shrug of her shoulders won the audience over.

McIntosh tried to win the audience back, and almost succeeded. He pointed to the Freudian theory that boys look for girls like their mothers to marry, ended his talk singing "I Want a Girl Just Like the Girl . . ."

The Exonian June 3, 1961

THE PHILLIPS EXETER ACADEMY, EXETER, N. H.   SATURDAY, DECEMBER 15, 1962   Ten Cents

Debaters Support Married Faculty; Instructors' Wives Remain at PEA

(L) Crowded into Daniel Webster Debating Room, students watch faculty wife-student debate. (R) Mrs. Jeffrey R. Fleischmann.

The Exonian December 15, 1962

Faculty Wives Find Opportunities at PEA; Praise Exeter Food, Students, Atmosphere

by Mark Waller

The life of an Exeter faculty wife is more pleasant than it may appear. From a survey taken last weekend, it appears that the life of a woman in a New England town can be as interesting and as stimulating as she cares to make it.

Mrs. Albert Ganley is very positive about the woman's life in a New England town like Exeter. "We are close enough to Boston to have some of the advantages of the city. At the same time we are far enough away to have the feeling we live in the country."

Mrs. Stephen Smith is not quite as enthusiastic about life in the middle of nowhere. Mrs. Werner Brandes would prefer to live closer to Boston so she could spend more time in the city. Mrs. Smith stays here most of the time largely because "it is too much trouble to get a baby sitter."

Faculty wives seem to be in complete accord in their praise for Exeter's merit as an educational institution. Mrs. K. Don Jacobusse thinks there "is a very good school atmosphere generally." She has met more young people that she could admire here than anywhere else. Mrs. Brandes, who is all for maximum exposure between students and faculty members and their families, also has great respect for the limited number of students whom she has met.

Faculty wives are generally very appreciative of dining hall food. Mrs. Jacobusse thinks "the food is very good except for the corn fritter things." When she and her husband came here from Germany, Mrs. Brandes thought "it was the best food I had ever eaten in my life."

Coeducation is one topic which is mutually interesting to the wives and to the students. Mrs. Jacobusse is strongly in favor of coeducation. Although she used to be for it but now is opposed, Mrs. Brandes thinks the lives of faculty wives would be much easier if Exeter were coeducational. Mrs. Smith is sure that "coeducation would ruin the school" and thinks that "the town of Exeter would go crazy with all those pretty girls around."

Mrs. Ganley is against coeducating because "as things are, there is a very solid feeling at Exeter and it may be a source of release for boys not to have girls always on their minds." She feels, however, that a sister school that is intelligently run would be marvelous.

Mrs. Smith echoes another common complaint when she says that "boys seem to think that we're here like trees." Mrs. Brandes agrees with this and sees a remedy to the situation in "greater inclusion of faculty wives in the life of the school."

"Faculty wives can make what they want out of school life," Mrs. Ganley says. She is presently a full time student at a local university majoring in English Literature.

However she believes that the great challenge to a wife at Exeter is "to maintain a home and family of her own."

The Exonian March 9, 1966

Chapter 9

Off Campus

From the mid-1930's to the middle of the 1960's women were not encouraged to work outside the home. This attitude was consistent with the norm of society at large. Consequently they found opportunities to use their talents by volunteering in a wide variety of ways.

The women enhanced scores of organizations that thrived through those decades. The League of Women Voters explored topics essential to an educated voter. Mary Thomas (1931), Tootie Cole (1947), Betty Brinckerhoff (1947), Van Moutis (1955), and Mary Echols (1957), to name but a few, honed their skills as researchers and orators preparing and presenting papers for the League meetings.

Betty and Van also volunteered for the Red Cross, along with Helen Stuckey who served as Executive Secretary and drove for the Motor Corps for thirty years. Helen also made radio broadcasts from the Portsmouth station in behalf of the National War Fund Chest. Van and Helen Clark served on Civil Defense standing on the water tower to spot airplanes in 1955 and 1956.

The performing arts benefited from the efforts of Academy people. The Exeter Players was founded in 1938 by faculty and their wives. Joan Lyford (1963) founded the Back Pack Players, a children's theater. Rosemary Coffin (1953) was a charter member of the Rockingham Choral Society, still in existence. Anne Gleason (1967) raised funds for the Boston Symphony and Betty Terry (1967) applied her skill as New Hampshire Chairman of the Friends of the Boston Symphony, and was awarded a prize for signing up the most new "friends."

The schools in town welcomed faculty wives in many ways. Lucy Weeks (1935) became Director of Guidance Services and received a Counselor of the Year Award from the State of New Hampshire. She also served on the board of the Group Home, a crisis center for troubled youth. Nancy Warren served as Principal of the Rockingham

School, a school for children with special needs, building on her training in Occupational Therapy and Physical Rehabilitation. Nancy Pierce (1971) and Dot Dunbar (1955) served as Director of Adult Education at the Exeter Area High School. Anne Gleason (1967) worked as a special education teacher in the public schools. Tootie Cole (1947) assisted in the kindergarten and ran a carpentry and sports program at the Exeter Day School, ran an Advanced Placement Program at PEA under a faculty supervisor, and volunteered in the elementary school, working in the library and tutoring in math.

The Exeter Day School hired many of the Academy wives as teachers: Tootie Cole (1947), Mary Fleischmann (1956), Ellie Tremallo (1964), Patty Heath (1947) and Shirley Brownell (1958), to name a few. Emily Cox (1948) taught kindergarten and later became Principal. In the late 1950's Emily and her sister-in-law, Pat Blair, sold hand-made articles at the Exeter Exchange Shop on Front Street near the bandstand.

Amanda Cilley (1864) helped to found the Exeter Hospital, and, years later, Jackie Thomas (1957) helped to organize the Volunteer Associates. Rosemary Coffin (1953) and Madeline Stuckey (1971) were instrumental in the founding of Hospice. Rosemary and David Coffin, Lois and Frank Gutmann (1963), and Ranny and LaRu Lynch (1939) worked for many years planning River Woods, a residential retirement community in Exeter.

The churches in town and the school church benefited from the ministrations of many wives. They visited the sick, sang in choirs, served on the vestry, worked with the youth, directed choirs and played the organ.

Van Moutis (1955) became active politically in the Exeter Women's Republican Club, serving on the State Committee. During the Nixon campaign of 1968, she organized activities for 200 high school and academy students. Isabelle Macomber was also very active in the Republican Party.

The Secret Lives Of Faculty Wives

Mrs. Cole   mjt

by James Figetakis

Although the Academy's male instructors may be seen conducting classes, plodding through papers and monotonously attending meetings, their female counterparts are just as busy carrying on their own pursuits and interests. The lines of work vary from law, which is practised by Mrs. Wharton, to physical therapy, by Mrs. Brewer, to many jobs involving Exeter as a community and Exeter as an educational institute.

Mrs. Cole was a faculty child herself who was raised most of her life in Exeter. For many years she has been a member of the Congregational Church, President of the League of Women Voters and a school volunteer, all which is attributed to her position on the school board of the Exeter School District. "We don't pretend to be professional educators," Mrs. Cole commented, "but public education in the United States has always had the input of its citizens."

Another locally involved woman, Mrs. Hoffman, counsels Junior High students. She is one of two counselors for nine hundred fifty students.

Mrs. Hoffman is also a member of the Exeter Area Youth Resource Team. "We take a look at what services are provided in the community for youth such as recreation, counseling and clergy." She also felt that it was good that the Academy has its own counseling service. Referring to her own counseling, she said, "We hope students will take a look at their self concept — how they see themselves — to help them feel worthwhile as people and realize their strengths."

As the first woman elected into the legislative General Court of Exeter, Mrs. Ganley has always been associated with politics. Her membership in countless political organizations gives her a strong-willed reputation. "I ran for legislator when I became involved in a fight with Aristotle Onassis involving an oil refinery which was to be built on Durham Point and The Isles of Shoals."

She is totally opposed to Governor Thomson's proposal of building five casinos to raise revenue with Hampton Beach as a likely site. She is also fighting the Seabrook Nuclear Plant. However, she admitted, "I have no qualms about attracting clean industry."

There are also two Exeter wives who are working on their degrees in literature in addition to instructing.

Mrs. Greer teaches at U.N.H. part-time while working for her master's in English. "I take a more than passing interest in Mr. Greer's work. We talk about literature and such." She feels this is healthy since "the demands on the faculty are so great that it is tremendously taxing and difficult for the instructor's spouse."

Mrs. Brandes, on the other hand, is working on her PhD in German Literature. She finds that "Harvard is a terrific place for a graduate student. However, it can be too big for an incoming, inexperienced undergraduate." She admitted she has Liza Knapp '75 in one of her classes and never knew her at Exeter.

Mrs. Brandes said that she was grateful to the Academy because she was able to audit Latin and French courses here. "This helped prepare me for exams at Harvard."

"I think the faculty spouses should feel more free to sit in on some courses to get a feeling of what students go through," she continued. "However, the school should take the initiative to invite them so that they don't feel like intruders."

Mrs. Brandes also said, "Society more and more does not press a woman into a mold but lets each one live out her own potential — anything from homemaker to a professional or artistic career."

Mrs. Brandes   Michael P. Sladden

The Exonian April 15, 1977

College alumnae like Betty Terry (1967) devoted many hours to the promotion of higher education. Betty was Class Agent for the 15th and 20th reunions, a member of the Alumnae Fund Committee, and Planned Giving Chair of her class at Smith College. As an attorney, Pat McKee Wharton (1975), sensitive to the inequalities of women under the laws and "rules" of society, specialized in the legal issues facing women.

Artists come in many guises. Helen Baker (Mrs. Henry Bragdon) (1945) and Alice Atkinson (Mrs. George C. Waterston) applied paint to canvas. Kit Cornell (1970's) is a potter, and Betty Terry (1967) creates needlepoint designs. Kathy Saltonstall wrote a book about their Peace Corps experience in Nigeria. Rosemary wrote two books: a biography and a novel.

Mrs. Bragdon's Paintings To Be Exhibited In Exeter

Two Faculty wives, Mrs. Henry W. Bragdon and Mrs. George C. Waterson, will give a public showing of their paintings. The exhibition will be shown in the Arts and Crafts Shop, located on Center Street, in Exeter.

Mrs. Bragdon, whose professional name is Helen Baker, is a graduate of the New School of Design in Boston. She also studied with the late Carl Caertner, of Cleveland, and with Carl Nelson, from Boston. Mrs. Bragdon has taught painting, and was assistant to Glen A. Krause, Director of the Lamont Art Gallery, until June of 1959.

Mrs. Bragdon has achieved her principal success in the realm of water color. "I like the freshness water colors give," she said. "The kind of painting I do is trying to catch the moment. I hope to convey my feelings to the viewer."

Mr. Bragdon stated of his wife's art, "It's impressionistic, I'd say — mostly."

The Boston Arts Festival accepted Mrs. Bragdon's work in 1952, 1953, and 1954. For two years running, she won the James C. Hill award given by the New Hampshire Art Association.

Mrs. Waterson, who paints under her maiden name, Alice Atkinson, was educated at the Museum School in Boston, the Art Students League in New York, and at the School of Fine Arts in Fontainbleau, France. She has taught art, and both her oil and watercolor work has been widely shown, in such places as Paris, Boston, New York, and various New England Galleries.

The exhibition will be made up of forty framed paintings, mostly watercolors, and a smaller number of paintings in portfolios.

November 30, 1960

Edible artistry was mastered by Ceci and Jim Samiljan who "have been unveiling their latest creations, but the shows don't last long. The audience eats the displays...their art is best suited to a galley than to a gallery." (Tim Norris, from *The Grapevine*)

Mrs. Samiljan Starts Bakery; Great Assortment Of Breads

by Melvin Coffee

The musty odors of the men's clothes of Chet's have been replaced by the engulfing aromas of Cecilia's Bakery specializing in European pastries and fine breads. Mrs. Cecilia Samiljan, faculty wife of James Samiljan, began operation in her new shop this Wednesday.

If you're expecting only the usual white and rye breads, you will be very pleasantly surprised by the enormous selection. Mrs. Samiljan offers all kinds of baked goods, including

challah, black, pumpernickel, cracked wheat, French, and raisin breads, in addition to fruit pastries, blueberry muffins, and a variety of cookies. But the list does not end here!

"I want to offer a variety of goods to the customers," said Mrs. Samiljan, "especially with the cookies." The assorted cookies may be purchased singly and by the dozen.

In addition to baked goods, Mrs. Samiljan offers various coffees from Columbia, Costa Rica, and a special blend of coffee beans from all over the world.

If at first you don't succeed...

This is not the first time that Mrs. Samiljan has thought of opening a bakery. She had long hoped to start her own business and the recent closing of Chet's enabled her to do so.

"I tried four years ago to open my own shop in town, but there was no space available," she said. "For two years I

Cecilia — Croissants, Rye, Amadama — so much for that diet... looked, but I just could not find anything. I had given up the idea until I learned that this location would be available."

Late Night Craving

Mrs. Samiljan also hopes to open a tea room to allow for a more relaxing atmosphere.

"I want to open it because I have the space." The room will be adjacent to the selling area and within the building.

Yet, Cecilia's extends itself further. Provided that orders are given in advance, Mrs. Samiljan will even bake and decorate cakes for special occasions.

The new bakery has already proved popular among residents of the town as well as Academy students. It is now open Tuesday through Friday, from 10:15 to 6:00. After Christmas vacation Cecilia's will be open from 7:30 to 9:00, Tuesday through Friday nights in order to satisfy those late night cravings.

Libby Bickel (1936) can still be seen visiting
the elderly and shut-in, a service of devotion
she has done for over 60 years. She has never
been one to sit still, constantly giving her
attentions to others.

There are three institutions which were
inspired and begun by faculty wives and
served the community at large. The Exeter Day
School, the Outgrown Shop, and the Child
Care Center.

Libby Bickel, Betsy Bickel
Hersam,   and   Ellen
Elizabeth Hersam. (Photo
courtesy of Libby Bickel)

The Exeter Day School: The First Twenty-two Years

Excerpts from a report written by Kathy Saltonstall
January 26, 1978

The Exeter Day School might be said to have been
conceived on a fine spring morning in 1934, as four young
Phillips Exeter Academy faculty wives [Marion Hatch,
Katharyn Saltonstall, Dorothy Smedley, and Mary
Thomas] watched their pre-school children playing in a
sandbox at 28 Pine Street in Exeter, New Hampshire, at
the home of Sherwood and Dorothy Smedley. As we chat-
ted, we discovered that we shared a deep conviction that
the elementary school years are the most important in the
educational process, for it is during one's first exposure to
school, whether in Nursery School or Kindergarten, First
Grade or the elementary grades which follow, that one's
attitude toward future learning is formed. The understanding and mastery of reading, writing, and arithmetic

and the application of these concepts to daily living is essential to the success of future learning.

We discovered that we wanted more for our children: social adjustments to other children and adults on a cooperative basis in an unpressured setting, flexible enough for individual children to proceed at their own pace. This was a tall order, almost impossible to carry out under the crowded conditions of the Court Street Elementary Public School even if the teachers wished to be flexible and innovative in their teaching. A rigid schedule was necessary because every classroom was overflowing and space in the cramped playground outside severely limited play. The prevailing philosophy that "what was good enough for our parents ought to be good enough for us and our children" provided an atmosphere that was hardly conducive to change. What could we do so that our children could benefit from some of the new ideas in elementary education that were being adopted in some of the independent schools in Boston and Cambridge? [Notably Shady Hill School, Cambridge MA.] The subject was fascinating to us, and we soon met again to discuss it further.

Marion Hatch, wife of Norman L., a member of the Latin department,...was a good worker, good at figures, long on enthusiasm. Dorothy Smedley, wife of Sherwood, a Chemistry teacher,...had a disciplined mind that could zero in on a problem, analyze the salient points, and come up with better suggestions and alternatives than anyone I have ever known. Mary Thomas, whose husband, Harris, was in the Academy French department, stood ready to take on any project providing it was challenging enough, and made light of the difficulties of raising enough money to start a school. The warmth of her heart and the soundness of her judgment became indispensable to the school during its first twenty years.

In 1936-37, 43 Pine Street was used for the first class of seven students. [This house was moved in 1964-5 to make way for the Episcopal Church. It now stands on Nelson Drive, behind the church.] The next year the Smedleys, 28 Pine Street, housed the 1st and 2nd grades.

In 1939 a newly formed Board of Trustees, selected the Marlboro Street location for their enrollment of twenty-six students. The Academy rented them the land for $1.00 per year. In the 1940's they provided grades Kindergarten to 4th grade. Later they added grade 5. When the new Elementary School was opened in 1951 there was less need for grades at the Day School and slowly the upper grades were dropped.

From *The Grapevine* of March 1966, an article on the Day School contained this additional information:

For the last two years Emily Cox, the school's ninth principal, has taught the kindergarten group; Ellie Tremallo has assisted her this year and Patty Heath will teach a second kindergarten made necessary by increased enrollment next year. Dee Fowler comes three mornings a week to work with small groups on special projects in the fields of science, art and carpentry. Mary Fleischmann also comes three mornings a week to bring the children a rich and varied diet of musical experiences. For the second year Betty Bates has had an experimental French group one morning a week with the kindergarten children.

Emily Cox and Christopher Hertig at the Day School. (Photo Courtesy of Shirley Brownell)

Emily Cox, Principal

Marta Snow, Trustee

The Outgrown Shop

The Outgrown Shop was formed to provide scholarships for Day School students. Bonnie Griswold (1950) describes the growth of the shop, beginning with the opening in 1953-54 in the Meras Store "two doors from Great Bridge on the Day School side of High Street. We sold 835 items to contribute $100 to the scholarship fund."

From High Street they moved into the Marlboro Street school basement. The shop was open on Fridays, and Tuesday the accounting session was held in Libby Niebling's kitchen and affectionately referred to as "the therapy" session. Each year they increased their contributions, reaching $2000 in 1976-77 from sale of 3,500 articles. The shop served two powerful purposes: to provide scholarships for students and to provide low-cost clothing for people in the community.

Child Care Center

Formal children's day care in Exeter began in 1975 as a branch of the Newmarket Day Care Center. Several Exeter parents were using the Newmarket facility because there was nothing in the town of Exeter. The Newmarket facility could not expand where it was and with the increasing demand from Exeter families, the Newmarket Day Care decided to open a satellite in Exeter. They rented the old Academy print shop with the generous $1.00 a year rental fee from the Academy. A *proviso* was attached: faculty children were to be assured entrance.

A group of volunteers refurbished the building, and the PEA maintenance department put in the required bathrooms and a chain link fence for the play yard. Joyce Morgan has pictures of their Puff the Magic Dragon float built for the 1975 Thanksgiving Day Parade. "Children are sitting around a seven foot tall papier mache Puff which we built in our Main Street apartment. It took up most of the living/dining room, and we glued-the-scales-on-the-dragon parties with other young faculty parents. It was a social event even before the parade."

In 1982 the Committee to Enhance the Status of Women (CESW) broached the idea of a Child Care Center for children of school employees. In the December 1982 CESW Newsletter, Bettye Pruitt reported that "for the time being the committee is looking for other ways to assist Academy employees in finding satisfactory daycare situations in the area. This information would help us to make an accurate assessment of the schools needs, as well as become the basis of a guide to finding child care. In addition, the committee hired a consultant who specializes in helping institutions respond to their employees' child-care needs."

Faculty wives who contributed to the research and formation of the Child Care Center include Amy Chartoff, Jeanne Kurtz, Snooky Mangen, Bettye Pruitt, Jackie Thomas, and Carol Tucker. The Center opened in 1988 in an apartment in the basement of Tan Lane House. The second principal was Snooky Mangan (1976). The facility expanded into more rooms in the Tan Lane house. In 1991 it moved to a building on Water Street.

Faculty wives found or made opportunities for their talents in addition to the time they spent with the the their families and Academy students. A list of the organizations in which they served or which they founded is only the beginning of understanding the impact these women had on the community as a whole.

Adult Education Director

American Field Service (AFS): started program in Exeter High School

Artists: painters, potters

Baker's Clay Ornament business

Boston Symphony Orchestra: Fund raiser

Boy Scouts

Cancer Society

Child and Family Services

Child Care Center

Churches: visit elderly, Sunday School Teacher, Altar Guild, choir member, organist, choir director, lay reader, vestry

Colonial Dames

Day Care Center: Charter member and co-founder

Teacher: Exeter and Durham High Schools

English Speaking Union

Exeter Day School: music teacher, teacher, Principal

Exeter Historical Society

Exeter Hospital: Nurses aide, Tumor Clinic, Nurses

Exeter Public Library: Children's Librarian

Exeter Players

Exeter Swim Team: long time supporter

Exeter Visiting Nurses: founder
FISH
Girl Scouts
Group Home for teens: founder
Guidance Counselor, Junior High School
Hospice
Hospital Volunteers
Lamaze Method of Prepared Childbirth
Lawyer
League of NH Crafters: window design
League of Women Voters
Needlepoint Design and Calligraphy Business
New Outlook Teen Center
Outgrown Shop
Parent Teachers Association
Politics: State and National
Psychiatric Social Worker
Red Cross: roll bandages, Motor Corps
Refugee Programs: brought Bosnian students to this country
Refugees: British children during W.W.II to PEA
River Woods: founder and trustee
Rockingham Choral Society: co-founder
Rockingham School
Save Our Shores (SOS)
Scouts
Seacoast Anti-Pollution League (SAPL)
Smith College: Alumnae Fund Committee, Class Agent
School Consultant
School Counselor
School Librarian
Special Education teacher
Speech Pathologist
Technical Secretary, UNH
Women Educators in Independent Schools Conference: office man-
    ager

Chapter 10

Women United

Beginning in the 1960's faculty wives sought more definition of their roles as well as more of a voice in the deliberations of the school in areas of community life. A variety of vehicles were created: The Sounding Board before coeducation, the P.E.A. Women because of coeducation, and the Committee to Enhance the Status of Women (CESW) after coeducation.

The Sounding Board 1964

In order to make Kathy Day's (1964) job as new Principal's wife easier, Jan Gillespie (1939) arranged for a group of wives to meet with Kathy upon her arrival in 1964. Originally known as "The Bag Lunch," it evolved into The Sounding Board, a committee of and for faculty wives chaired by Kathy Day and including Rosemary Coffin, Marta Snow, Barbara Hoffman, Linda Mahoney, Janice Hanson and Nancy Pierce. "The Sounding Board exists to serve the distaff side of the community, and welcomes our suggestions, questions, problems, and plain ol' gripes." (*The Grapevine* September 1972)

P.E.A.Women 1974

The first meeting of the P.E.A. Women was in October of 1974, four years into coeducation. Its purpose was to have small groups that were representative of the interests and skills of *all* PEA women and a larger group which would provide the opportunity to get together as a community. (*The Grapevine* XII.2.) There was a large and enthusiastic turnout, and the number of sign-ups for the small interest groups was most gratifying. One of the larger projects involved meeting with the wives of both Andover Academy and St. Paul's School in an effort to learn how women fared at other independent schools as faculty, staff, and faculty spouses.

Committee to Enhance the Status of Women(CESW) 1982

The CESW came into being in response to an anonymous gift of money "to assist with obtaining, or improving the role of, significant women on the faculty of Phillips Exeter Academy." In making this gift the donor, a parent of an Exeter graduate, cited the importance of providing role models among the faculty—professional women whose accomplishments would inspire girls to strive to develop their talents and establish their own professions.

The initial efforts of this committee concentrated on faculty women, their housing and their professional encouragement. The first issue of the CESW newsletter, April 1982, reported on a three-day symposium by the human-relations consultant, Edith Seashore of Washington, D.C., a specialist in the problems of integrating women into traditionally male institutions. She met with faculty women, faculty wives and clerical staff. She shared her observations pertaining to the faculty wives:

> "Twenty-two women attended the meeting held for faculty wives who live in dormitories....Most of these women have careers of their own and no longer feel a vital part of the dormitory. But they consider themselves to be a valuable resource for the Academy. They also feel that for what they contribute they receive very little thanks or recognition. The wives feel they could provide role models for female students and be an important resource to the community." (CESW Vol. 1, Number 2)

In another series of discussions involving faculty women the concern voiced was that "spouses were not able to compete for tenure-track appointments on an equal footing with outsiders, though they were welcomed as temporary help in an emergency situation." The response from the Heads of Departments was that spouses would be treated equally, but consideration had to be given to dormitory staffing problems(CESW February 1983).

Faculty Wives Sub-committee
(Anne Campbell, Carol Hamblet, Patty Heath, Wendy Hitzrot)

This committee was formed around 1984 to focus attention on the issues which involve faculty families at Exeter. In particular, they were concerned with the quality of life of the residential faculty as well as the Academy community as a whole.

In 1985 this committee organized a series of dessert parties for all faculty, spouses and local emeriti. Eight gatherings were held, and judging from the positive responses received, provided an opportunity for members of the Academy family to socialize and share ideas. These dessert parties were reminiscent of the after-dinner gatherings of the 1930's and 1940's. The committee also sponsored a discussion of the special pressures of being a faculty child *and* Academy student.

Women and Physical Activity

One consistent problem was the use of the gymnasium by both wives and faculty women. Before coeducation the wives used the old locker room below Thompson Gymnasium. The major activity available was the use of the old swimming pool at a time when the students were not using the lockers, the showers, or the pool.

After coeducation Kathy Conway, Director of Physical Education, wrote in *The Grapevine*, September 1973: "All female faculty, or faculty wives not directly involved in the athletic program...are asked to use the locker room one floor below the girls' locker room..." [This locker room was below pool level, next to the boys' Varsity Swim Team locker room. One wife was startled when a door to her locker room opened, and the boys' enjoyed a glimpse of her dressing. That was the last time she used that locker room.]

The Grapevine, December of 1974, ran this article: Ladies Gym Night: The gym continues to be open for Academy Women 7-10 PM on

Tuesday night. If you like to play volleyball, come at 7:30; swimming is from 8:00-9:00, and squash is anytime. Please come if you can, as only continued enthusiasm can make this effort worthwhile.

Joan Lyford recalls going to swim on a cold morning.

> Wives wanted to use the gym and swim in the pool. After much negotiation we were given 8:30-9:30 a.m. Tuesday mornings to swim. All swimmers supported it even though it was a ghastly time. One cold February morning I found myself over at the pool alone. Of course I went for my swim. But Kathy got a call from Nick Moutis that I had been observed ALONE! Nothing had been said about a "buddy system." The next time I went swimming Nick came down to the pool to speak with me. But I just kept swimming back and forth in the middle of the pool until he got frustrated and left! Thus the pool got integrated!

> Ten years later, in 1983, the locker room space was still at a premium.

> In an attempt to accommodate everyone, we are installing some temporary lockers in the girls' locker room. These will be assigned on a first-come, first-serve basis. Women are encouraged to use the separate adult female locker room for showering and changing if so desired. Please, however, keep children in the girls' (or boys') locker room only.

> Our hope is that some day we will have the resources to expand the facility for all our academy females. In the meantime we hope this will help.(CESW May 1983)

Using the gym facilities was one way for the women to feel a part of the campus, and many women did participate. Since physical education was emphasized for students and faculty, it seemed appropriate for the faculty wives and families to be encouraged as well.

Chapter 11

The Grapevine

The Grapevine (1965-1977) was a comprehensive newsletter designed to impart information about the larger community and about campus activities. The idea for *The Grapevine* grew out of a feeling that the Academy community had increased to such a size that the sense of closeness that had been evident among the faculty and staff in the past was slipping away. The quarterly newsletter was a way to provide information for new faculty about the Exeter area, Durham to Boston, as well as introduce the faculty and staff to each other. The first issue in April of 1965 set forth the aim of the publication:

> *The Grapevine* is to be mainly an information service for faculty wives and their families. We hope to publish about four times a year and maintain a bulletin board outside the Perry Room [a room in the back of One Abbot Place, the former Principal's House, used by the faculty wives for coffees, teas and gatherings]."

We shall provide information on:

1. Art exhibits, concerts and theater in Exeter, Durham, Manchester and Boston.

2. Opportunities for part-time employment in the Academy and elsewhere and for community service in organizations like

the Red Cross, Bixler House, Scouting, the Exeter Hospital and the Seacoast Family Service.

3. Skills and services offered by wives and members of their families and equipment for sale or rent.

4. Formal and informal leisure-time activities, classes, and reading groups.

5. Sports.

6. Rides to Boston, Durham, or ski centers and other travel information.

We shall also carry news, announcements and editorials concerning Academy life. Let us know if you have any further suggestions for ways *The Grapevine* could be useful, or ideas that you would want to have included.

The women whose names appear on this first issue are Helen Barry, Barbara Burgin, Eleanor Dunnell, Helena Finch, Bonnie Griswold, Libby Niebling, Mary Swift, and Margot Trout. For subsequent issues, there were as many as 20 women working as editors, reporters, and typists.

A wide variety of articles were printed about the wives' experiences. Here are excerpts from articles printed over the life of the paper.

The Spur Program, by Patricia Heath

During the winter of 1963-64 the Phillips Exeter Academy planned to expand its scholarship program of the Summer School to include a special scholarship program for urban boys and girls who had completed the 8th grade, who had achieved good scores, and who had shown evidence of a strong desire to improve themselves and their education. There were several unique features of this program, called SPUR. The selection was made by the school authorities in the local schools of the participating cities. Faculty-Observers accompanied these students, and the students were only a small part of a Summer School of almost 400 students from 42 different states. Although there are 115 colleges with programs similar to Exeter's, our school is the only secondary school where these students are integrated totally in the dormitory, classroom, and in the recreational life of the school.

(June 1965)

SYA in Barcelona by Lois Gutmann

"...When we first arrived in Barcelona, we lived in one room in a rather picturesque pension called the Ramos. While we were at the Ramos, I really had little to do since we ate all of our meals in the main dining room with the other residents. In many ways this was nice as it gave me a lot of free time to take Spanish lessons and to roam about the shopping districts and the narrow streets of "the old city." I also met a fascinating elderly English lady and her husband who were permanent residents of the Ramos. They and their families had lived in Spain for many, many years and told most interesting and exciting stories of life in Barcelona before and during the Civil War..."

(October 1968)

A poem by Lilja Rogers (April 1965)
Ole!

My husband's gone to Spain on a sabbatical.
"A teacher's Spanish must be idiomatical,"
he told me, and he said it quite emphatical
but he is neither senile nor sciatical.

"Travel is to me anathematical,
besides a pet keeps one at home dogmatical,"
I told our friends—one must be diplomatical,
The reason I stayed home was mathematical.

But now I'll *swim* to Spain, although it's problematical
That I'll arrive because I'm unaquatical;
However, jealousy will make my strength fanatical.
His latest letter, was it idiomatical?
Uh, uh—ecstatical.

Lilja Rogers, published in
The Independent School Bulletin, May 1961

Rennes SYA by Carol Hamblet

...I often think back of the sounds which were familiar during the first three months of our residence in Villejean, Rennes, France...Monsieur Denis owns the Boulangerie where the delivery trucks from Le Grand Moulin arrive about 6:20 a.m. with flour and other bakery products...It's time to get out of bed when the "buurrhh" of Madame Simon's coffee grinder can be heard, grinding the first coffee for the morning café.   (November 1974)

A Trip to Russia by Andrea Deardorff

...One of the first observations we made is that there appear to be few Soviet women who fall into the 30-50 age category. Yes, they are there, but life is such that a woman who is thirty has the appearance of being fifty. This, we feel, is the result of a life of hard work, inadequate diet, and a lack of cosmetics.... The typical Soviet housewife works outside the home. She will have to arrive home after her day's work, do her shopping, and prepare the evening meal. The shopping is a long process because of the ever-present line. A shopper first stands in line to make her choice, then stands in line to pay for her purchase, and then must go back to wait for an opportunity to break into the line, present her sales-slip, and receive her purchase. This process must be repeated numerous times—nearly as frequently as the number of items that are being purchased.   (October 1975)

"*With a Soft Voice*" by Anne Cunningham

An Academy senior said, "You have no idea how strange it is to have someone teaching Mathematics with a soft voice!" Then there was the Fac Brat...,"You are the lady teacher, aren't you? What do you teach?" "<u>Mathematics</u>—I thought you taught English or History—Mathematics—whee-e!" And he fell backwards off the wall...

Why did I come to teach at P.E.A.? The reason is quite simple: I have taught for several years in one of the best public schools in the country and wanted to teach in what I now know to be one of the best private schools. That I am also the first woman full-time faculty member at The Phillips Exeter Academy means much to me personally...[I]t is not only logical but even essential that our young women use to the fullest their intellectual endowment, even in math and sciences. (June 1969) [Ann was hired to teach for one year prior to coeducation in 1970.]

Congratulations Due:
    ...Joan Lyford and Dorothy Thorp for their performances in student Vincent De Santis' musical version of "High Tor."
    ...Mid Adkins for her direction of, and Nancy Heyl for her performance in, the recognition scene from "Anastasia," given in the One Act Play Competition for the Seacoast Area. (June 1965)

A Welcome to New Faculty Wives from Kathy Day, a year after becoming Principal's wife.
    Last year at this time, I was the newest and greenest of 'new wives' so I sympathize with the mixture of pleasure, excitement, and confusion that some of you must be feeling. Actually, only a 'new wife' would make that statement in the first person singular, for the truth is all wives have been through the same bewildering first days at Exeter..... (September 1965)

New Academy Library by Ned Echols
    Those young ladies who take their assigned places in the Assembly Hall in September will find themselves in overwhelmingly masculine company, actual and portrayed. But over the front entrance on the west side of the Hall they will see a single feminine portrait, whose elevated location will make the title plate impossible to read. The title plate does in fact read: Mrs. Charlotte J.G. Sibley, Benefactress. Mrs. Sibley's place of honor is rightfully hers, for none have given to the Academy a greater share of what they owned than she and her husband... (September 1970)

Things that were going on

The Infirmary Visiting: A committee of wives who volunteer to go to the Infirmary and take a tray of orange juice around to the students and offer smiles, etc. has been discontinued on a regular, daily basis. Dr. Heyl, however, would like to encourage a home-like atmosphere in the Infirmary. It has been suggested that Faculty Wives might pay a friendly visit to their husband's advisees, when they are ill...

(September 1965)

Reading Group: William Faulkner's *Light in August*. Andrea Deardorff will give the author's background...

(September 1965)

Other groups:
Foods and Moods, Speaker's Forum, Social Functions, Book discussion, *The Grapevine*, Gym Night, Student Contact, Public School volunteers, Bread making, Language group, Dorm Life and Crafts.

With so many opportunities to cook for the students, it was natural for wives to share their favorite and most popular recipes. These are a very small sample from *The Grapevine*.

<u>Recipes</u>

Cocoa for a Crowd (serves 60) Tootie Cole, Pat Heath
Hot Spiced Tea (25 cups) Marta Snow
Punch (65-70) Elizabeth Compton
Hot Spiced Cider (serves 40-50)
Nancy Warren, Elizabeth Compton

Refreshments Ideas for a Large Dorm (serves 65 boys)
Sue Wilson

2 gallons ice cream
4 double batches cookies
8 angel food cakes
Soda pop from Connor Bottling Co.—1 case orange, 2 assorted.
This is a nice change from the coke machine.
Mr. Connor will pick up and deliver.
Try his golden ginger ale—it is delicious!

Brownies for a crowd (makes 56) Nancy Warren
Grinders (for 15 boys) Nancy Warren

A Dance Weekend Breakfast for 12 Couples
Nancy Warren, Elizabeth Compton

(In 1967 or so this cost approximately $1.25 per couple)
orange juice
2 gallons milk
coffee (30-40 cups)
3 dozen eggs
6 pounds ham, or 4 pounds sausage, or 3 pounds bacon
4 packages English muffins
pound butter
jam-jelly
pint cream

The End of *"The Grapevine"*

October of 1977 saw the final issue of *The Grapevine*. The staff of eight felt that unless there was a positive mandate for it to continue, it would cease publication.

> Going, going—GONE? YES, *The Grapevine* will cease publication—UNLESS there is a positive mandate for it to continue. Perhaps it no longer fills the need felt for it in the past. Some of the information it has carried now appears in other notices and listings of campus events.

Many women edited, produced, and approached people to contribute articles including profiles, recipes, items for the calendar of events, places to shop, and events at the school. They worked faithfully from 1965 to 1977 with a deep commitment to the community, fulfilling a real need. No one came forward to be an editor, co-editor, writer or interviewer. The newsletter had contributed to a sense of community as the school grew in size and became coeducational. No other publication arose to take its place.

Chapter 12

Greasepaint, Tutus and Celluloid

Drama and Dance

Faculty wives, active in both school and community theater acted, made costumes, taught, applied makeup, and directed. Some of the funnier stories about the women and theater on campus come before coeducation when wives acted in school productions and made costumes for the all-male casts.

A Mouthful of Hairpins[4]
The Theater at Exeter in 1926-27
By Henry C. Friend '27

In 1926-1927 the theater at the Phillips Exeter Academy was not conducted by a club or organization but by the Academy itself. The presiding genius was Frank Cushwa, Chairman of the English Department. He chose the plays to be performed and the casts of characters, while responsibility for the actual stage direction fell to Earl Alonzo Barrett, who taught French. Mr. Barrett was clever and had an excellent sense of timing. Although the Academy was then a boys'

---

4 From the Academy Archives, E Urm 1927 F

school, Mr. Cushwa chose plays in which the leading characters were women.

In 1926 his choice was Anatole France's play, "The Man who Married a Dumb Wife," and the role of the wife was played by Arthur Knox '26. Arthur Knox was a small boy with a pleasant voice. When he wore street clothes, he tended to conform to the character and appearance of other small boys, and was not particularly distinguished.

As the wife he wore a conical medieval woman's hat which was about a foot and a half tall and draped with cloth, as was his costume. His bearing and demeanor were warm and ingratiating, as was his voice. By virtue of his conical hat, he was able to lord it over Courtland Hill, Edward Cilley Wiest and most of the other members of the cast, who were actually taller than he was. Since I was six feet tall and wore medieval physician's cap and gown, Arthur and I were well proportioned.

Mr. Cushwa's next inspiration was to cast his neighbor, Mrs. John C. Kirtland, as 'Apple Mary' in a play which he may have chosen as a vehicle for her....

Mrs. Kirtland usually stayed in the background and was popularly supposed to devote her time primarily to the care of the Kirtland household and to the rearing of the numerous Kirtland children. As Apple Mary, she dressed in shabby clothing, bustled about the stage, which she dominated, and showed herself to be a talented character actress, full of brown-eyed intelligence.

While this casting was regarded as evidence of Mr. Cushwa's perceptive intuition, the casting of "Three Wise Fools," the principal play for the year 1927, was obvious. The part of the ingénue went to the wife of Percy Rogers, who taught French and was the Academy tennis coach. Mrs. Rogers [Lil Rogers], who was reported to have married at the age of 18, was lithe and often went about in a tennis dress. In the community at Exeter, where people greeted each other on sight and the atmosphere was friendly, Mrs. Rogers tended to be aloof and to befriend primarily those boys for whom her husband acted as tennis coach or adviser. As she passed, she was usually alone, would walk rapidly and when the students saluted her with wolf calls and wolf whistles, she took no notice as though she had not heard them. None the less, if anyone asked an Exeter student whether he would prefer to see Ginger Rogers, the motion picture actress, or Lil Rogers, act the part of the ingénue, he would have replied "Lil Rogers." This was his opportunity to hear her speak and to see what she was like.

The play was performed in the chapel of the Academy Building, a room equipped with a stage and benches for the entire school. When the bell in the steeple was rung, the room would vibrate and shake. On the evening of the performance every bench was occupied.

The three wise fools were elderly men, and the parts were played by George Phillips, E. Tremaine Bradley, and by me. The action of the play called for me to kiss the ingénue, and when Mrs. Rogers came to me, I sought to kiss her. All that I got was a mouthful of hairpins. However, the audience was under the illusion that I had kissed her, and this brought the house down, so that the Academy building reverberated with enthusiastic applause.

> We were prurient little boys who used to gaze admiringly out the window of Abbot Hall when the luscious wives of Dexter Butterfield, a mathematics' teacher, and Percy Rogers, a French master, passed below.
>
> Class of 1930 50th Reunion notes

Lilja Rogers with Percy, son Brandon and Dog 1929
(Photo courtesy of Brandon Rogers)

"Wasn't Percy Rogers' wife beautiful? And the blonde daughter of the coach. Now THOSE were memories!"

Class of 1930 50th Reunion notes

When Violette Bennett helped out with theater productions they were held in the Assembly Hall in the Academy Building. She played Lady Macbeth, about which she said, "I hate to think back on that." When the boys played the girls' parts, she would size up the boys and then go to her friends to find appropriate clothes. If a special costume needed to be rented, she went to Hooker and Howe costume rental house in Haverhill, Massachusetts, which was very time consuming as Route 95 was not built yet. Play rehearsals were often held on Sundays, the only day off for George.

Once, when a large-sized student came to Susan Wilson's living
room to be fitted for a costume he
refused to unbuckle his pants for her
to measure his waist. She had to
guess his measurement and used
elastic. When it came time for the
performance Susan went over to the
Academy Building to help with costumes and was amazed to find the
boys running around in their shorts
without any hesitation. Ironically, the
football players took the parts of the
girls; the skinny boys played the men.

Rosemary Coffin, Gene Finch
and Ted Scott applying make-up
for a school production. (Photo
courtesy of Rosemary Coffin)

Joan Lyford came to Exeter in 1963
with an extensive background in the-
ater: Child Drama and Children's Theater at UNH, Multi Arts, Drama
in Education, and Alternative Music. At the Academy she was active in
Dramat as an actress. She assisted Rod Marriott in teaching three
courses: Theater History, Acting and Play Writing. She created her own
Child Drama and Children's Theater program, Backpack Players, and
later, Project Blue Sky, for the Lincoln St. School.

Joan wrote:

> Contrary to some opinions the Dramat was one of the most
> important places of learning outside of rowing a shell. It was
> the only place where cooperation was absolutely necessary in
> order for a production to take place. It allowed expression of
> feeling, experience, personal responsibility to the group and
> resulted in hard work. I knew some students who felt they
> had to choose between being in a play or failing their classes
> that semester. It was the only place where students felt a sense
> of community. The fact that the Academy did not see itself as
> a community was its greatest failure in my estimation.
> Departments did not interact but were very territorial. Dick
> Day once said to me, "That Dramat. It's a thorn in my side."
> To which I replied, "I'd like to remind you, Dick, that thorns
> have roses.

Occasionally faculty wives were asked to teach a section or two. One "glorious" (Nancy Heyl's word) year Rob Marriot had too big a senior class in drama and asked Joan Lyford and Nancy Heyl to each take a third section and share the class.

Theater in town: The Exeter Players

In 1938 Academy faculty members founded the Exeter Players, an amateur community theater group that involved community people, many faculty, and their wives. With no theater of its own they performed in a variety of halls: the Unitarian Church, the Episcopal Church (when it was on Eliot Street), the Town Hall and a barn in Newfields.

"The Importance of Being Earnest," performed in 1949, featured Sue Carhart as Lady Bracknell. Rebecca Hogg, who appeared for the first time on an Exeter stage, "did a skillful job in her inimitable characterization of Miss Prism." Newcomer Emily Cox was Gwendolyn Fairfax.

Emily Cox and Bob Lucky in *The Importance of Being Earnest*, 1949 (Exeter Historical Society)

E. Wood and Rebecca Hogg
in *The Importance of Being
Earnest*, 1949
(Exeter Historical Society)

In "Blithe Spirit" Harry Leighton played the husband Charles. The spirit of his first wife was played by his own wife, Doris. Rebecca Hogg as Madame Arcati, the medium, had the "fattest" part in the play. This eccentric character was given a superb going-over by Mrs. Hogg, "who missed none of the rich opportunities." Susan Wilson and Constance Hatch worked backstage and Pam Krause designed the set.

The Sunday afternoon Gilbert and Sullivan (G&S) Teas were organized by Ted Scott, English teacher, who had been on the stage in England doing G & S. He shared his enthusiasm with the community by directing readings and sing-alongs in the Alumni Hall. Ted performed the patter songs and directed the chorus. Libby Bickel and others remember these productions as a wonderful social event, enjoyed by many.

Susan Wilson, S Carhart, and Van Moutis in *Gigi*, 1961.
(Exeter Historical Society)

Sally Bissell and Ranny Lynch in *Angel Street*, 1948
(Exeter Historical Society)

Nancy Heyl and Bob Luckey in *Joan of Lorraine*
(Exeter Historical Society)

Violette Bennett on the right in *Holiday*, 1940.
(Exeter Historical Society)

A.Travato and Louise Funkhouser in *Laura*, 1951
(Exeter Historical Society)

Dave Thomas, left; Jackie Thomas, seated
center, and Rosemary Coffin, standing right,
in *Reluctant Debutante*, 1959
(Exeter Historical Society)

The Big Screen

In 1947 Nancy Heyl acted in a "March of Time" film, *Lost Boundaries*, with Mel Farrer. Soon after the film was released, Nancy hosted a new wife at a Newcomer's Tea. Nancy introduced the new wife to the faculty wives as they came in. The wives acknowledged the new wife briefly, then turned to Nancy and raved about her performance in the movie. It was quite embarrassing for Nancy and for the new wife.

In the Spring and Summer of 1971, Hollywood brought its "glitz" to campus and lured Rebecca Hogg (1931) and several other wives into serving tea on screen in *A Separate Peace*, based on the novel by John Knowles. Rebecca's daughter, Margaret Upham (1944) remembers her mother enjoying the experience of recreating the teas that she herself served to the boys in the school in the 1940's.

In July 1971 *The Boston Globe* described it this way: "As for Mrs. John C. Hogg of Exeter, whose husband for thirty years taught science at the Academy, she wore the very same beautifully made gown of silver gray and dark brown silk, with a handsome mantilla (she called it a fascinator) she wore in 1942...Enjoying tea with her were a group of seven faculty wives who 'walked, laughed, conversed and took their tea as if to the manner born...'"

On Broadway

Though no wives ended up on a Broadway stage, Robert Anderson of the class of '35 immortalized the school in his play *Tea and Sympathy*. Mr. Anderson wrote to the *Exeter Bulletin* in the Spring of 1997 in response to Katherine Towler's article about women on campus before coeducation. In his letter he remembers revisiting Williams House, where he had been a proctor his senior year. Harris Thomas and his wife, Mary, Anderson's former dorm parents, were still living in the dorm. They welcomed him, and two movie producers, into their home as they absorbed the atmosphere of the school and the dorm.

After the play came out on Broadway, believing the play may have offended sensibilities, Mr. Anderson wassurprised to be invited to give a library talk. The Thomases again invited him to their home, this time for a small party. As he entered the house, he took Mrs. Thomas aside and said, "I hope the play hasn't caused you any embarrassment." She replied, "Nobody has been so kind as to suggest that I was the woman!"

Dance: Learning left from right

Dance became a course of study at the Academy through the efforts of two faculty wives. In the 1930's square and contra dancing were introduced and made popular by Barbara Little. Her efforts were thought by many on campus to be revolutionary.

Forty years later another wife led a student folk dance group, which met once a week either in the old gym or in the Elting Room. Trustee Ottaway gave money for a studio dance floor to be installed in a left-over room in the basement of the old gym. As dance became a recognized course of study, a dance studio was built in the gymnasium and dance became part of the physical education program.

Dance, which had reinforced the feeling of community, was joined by another artistic expression: "The Bicentennial Quilt."

The Bicentennial Quilt

Excerpts from a summary written by Carol Hamblet and Pam Parris:

In the Spring of 1979 faculty wives Carol Hamblet and Pam Parris sent out about 300 letters to friends of the Academy inviting them to meet and begin work on a quilt to celebrate the Bicentennial of the school. The final design, inspired by Rebecca Dunham, placed twenty-two squares around a central large square depicting the Academy seal. It provided an opportunity for 125 men and women from all segments of the Academy community—Emerti, faculty, students, staff, spouses and children—to work together on a unique gift to the school.

(Photo courtesy of Academy Archives)

At the end of April in 1980 a sewing marathon began. Mornings, afternoons, and evenings were spent arranging the squares, assembling the top, and basting batting and backing together. The final quilting could begin. Each quilter of a square invited three or four new people to participate, including people who had never held a needle before. In total, thirty-eight people designed and stitched the squares.

The last weekend was hectic. It seemed like people came out of the walls to sew a few stitches—entire families, friends, children, and in-laws all arrived to take part. Sunday afternoon three sunbathing students gave up their tans to put the finishing stitches on the quilt. The schedule was met—the Quilt was complete on June 1st. The novice stitchers (only two had made a quilt before) who worked diligently for months had produced a professional quilt in one hundred and two days.

On June 3, 1980, the Quilt was presented to Principal Stephen Kurtz and Assistant Principal Henry Bedford. The Quilt, when not on display at events during the Bicentennial Celebrations, was displayed at the Exeter Inn.

(The Quilt is on permanent display in the corridor outside the History Department Room on the first floor of the Academy Building.)

Chapter 13

The Envelope, Please

The Founder's Day Award, presented at a student assembly in the Spring, was established in 1976 by Principal Kurtz to recognize exceptional service to the Academy. Six faculty wives have been so honored: Katharyn Saltonstall, Helen Stuckey, Jeanne Kurtz, Rosemary Coffin, Shirley Brownell, and Barbara James. Following are the award presentations and the responses of some of the recipients.

Katharyn Watson Saltonstall
Recipient of Founder's Day Award 1981

Mother of five, friend and counselor to the Academy family, wife of a Principal, and a lady for all seasons, Katharyn Watson Saltonstall brought humanity, warmth, wisdom and grace to the life of Phillips Exeter and the Town of Exeter.

Katharyn Watson Saltonstall came to Phillips Exeter in 1932, at a time when the Academy was a school for boys taught by men. At first, like other wives, she lived in a dormitory from where she quietly reached out with graciousness to the students and other faculty and their wives. She was unpretentious but vibrant, self-effacing but sensitive to all about her.

When Bill became Principal, Kathy truly became the principal faculty wife—First Lady to faculty and staff and their families. She became the prototype for other wives, setting an example of commitment, accepting uncomplainingly the demands made on her. She opened her home to all, but still managed to reserve a portion of her life for her family. She raised five children, of whom the two boys attended the Academy. In addition, she was able to be, and not just appear to be, the available mother, the daughter, the older sister, or the younger sister, the principal listener and sympathizer to countless boys, faculty, faculty wives, and children who attended Exeter for one, four, or 40 years.

In her contacts with people in the community, Kathy was warm and genuine. She shared her friendship with town and gown, faculty and staff. She knew all the faculty, their wives and children—even their dogs.

Kathy brought a selfless dedication to important little things like planting daffodil bulbs at Phillips Church in memory of a boy killed in Korea, or calling on a new faculty wife in Amen, or taking over her son Sam's paper route, or consoling a custodian's widow, or cofounding the Exeter Day School, or running the Red Cross drive, or knitting a sweater for a new baby. It was Kathy's dedication that made Exeter a warmer place for everyone at a time when life at the Academy was reputed to be cold.

When called to Exeter in 1932, she came. When called to Nigeria in 1963, she went. Whither her husband went, there she went also. Whatever he did, she supported and helped him.

At Exeter Kathy's wisdom, warmth, and loyalty made her the model of an ideal partner. She still is.

A Bicentennial Founder's Day Award is richly deserved by Kathy Saltonstall.

Helen Potter Stuckey '22(Hon.) and '30(Hon.)
Recipient of Founder's Day Award 1982

For sixty-five years now you have been the most remarkable of Exonians. The wife of one distinguished faculty member and the mother of another, you have watched one son and five grandsons graduate from the Academy; you have become, by adoption, the only woman member of the Classes of 1922 and 1930; and you have made yourself the honorary mother to countless Exeter students. Perhaps the greatest accolade the academy can bestow has already been given you: at nearly every alumni reunion a procession of graduates makes its way down Front Street to pay homage at your house on Gilman Lane.

What other woman of retirement age is still so immersed in her school and community? Every Wednesday and Friday you select and arrange the flowers for Phillips Church, the parish you joined upon first coming to Exeter in 1917. On Thursdays you tutor adults for their high school equivalency diplomas. And almost every Wednesday and Saturday in term find you over at the gym or on the playing fields, cheering on the Academy teams with more athletic perspicacity than most of the faculty could muster.

One of your grandsons has written of you: 'She has never seemed an older person to me. She is old, but not older. She can tell me what life was like in the Academy in 1917, but coming from her it is like my friend telling me what it is like living in Abbot Hall as a senior. The past is fresh in her presence; she makes my view of today broader and deeper.'

There is no part of this Academy, just as there is none among many generations of alumni, that has not been touched by your warmth and gentle wisdom. You touch us still, for your joy in living your eighty-eighth year is obviously no less than the enthusiasm you brought to your twenty-third. You show us what, if we were very fortunate, we too might become.

Steve and Jeanne Kurtz
Recipients of Founder's Day Award 1987

You, Steve Kurtz, conceived the Founder's Day Award. It is fitting that at the conclusion of your principalship at Exeter you receive the award. The only proviso is that you share it officially, equally, gratefully, and unabashedly with Jeanne.

Even though you, Jeanne Kurtz, have earnestly pursued your own separate career in classics at the University of New Hampshire, you have been a true partner of your husband in his tenure as Principal. You have been the hostess and spouse, the support system, the one who calmed him when he waxed emotional. You have laughed at his jokes, and have given good counsel, content to know and not to broadcast who really minded the store.

You two together, Steve and Jeanne, are indeed responsible for the era of good feeling, that in the last thirteen years, has blessed this Academy...

The open secret of your magic with students is that you like them and they know it. It is not possible to hide condescension and distrust of the young, and you have none to hide. One would not think it possible for a Principal and a Principal's spouse to befriend 980 students at a time; but somehow, despite your finite time, you have done so. Your sensitivity, humor, and goodwill have convinced students that your friendship is always available. By your famous open houses, by your faithful attendance at sports events, including club and prep games, and at exhibitions, plays, concerts, and services, and in a host of less obvious ways, you have shown that you cared. You are both still seventeen!

You have observed and affected all but the very beginning of coeducation at Exeter. Though there have been problems along the way, you deserve the credit for the progress that has been made. Consistently and without exception you have promoted the equality of girls and boys and women to men, a status that has all but been achieved today. You have thus paved the way and are the fitting predecessors for the Principal-elect and her spouse. Though some may always question change and argue the loss of this standard or that, all agree that the Academy is a nicer, warmer, more humane place than it was thirteen years ago. Perhaps this is because the girls and women arrived; surely it was because you arrived…

Jeanne and Steve Kurtz, you brought to Exeter a love of people and an abiding respect for youth. On this Founder's Day, this 15th day of May, 1987, we honor you together with the Founder's Day Award, in gratitude for the love and respect you have left with us to share with all future Exonians.

Rosemary Honor Coffin
Recipient of Founder's Day Award 1990

In one of Frost's most daringly beautiful sonnets, he compares an extraordinary woman to a silken tent set in a field—"She is as in a field a silken tent..." We should claim this poem for Rosemary Honor Baldwin Coffin because *she* is an extraordinary woman and because she, like the woman in Frost's poem, is "bound/By countless ties of love and thought/To everything on earth the compass round." For many years the Academy was happily the center of Rosemary Coffin's inclusive love.

She had regular open houses for the boys in the dorm. These wonderful occasions were always upbeat because as Rosemary has said, the young prefer "hamburgers and humor to tea and sympathy." She made about two hundred birthday cakes and gave parties for the same number of birthdays in the dorm; she regularly visited students in the infirmary; and when she and David moved out of the dorm, she invited students in David's Greek and Latin classes to dinner at least once a semester.

Her loyalty to, and her love of, the Classics Department extended to typing endless section lists for posting at the beginning of school; to housing and feeding a long series of visiting speakers for the Kirtland Society; to making up displays for the department's bulletin board— especially memorable were selections of cartoons on the Trojan Horse from *Punch* and *The New Yorker*.

She continues strong and powerful in her conviction that we live to care for one another. Her infectious smile and her earthy laughter, her devotion to her garden, her private attention to her writing—whether full-length biography or novel—never blur her singular vision of why we are here: to love God in loving, and in ministering to our sisters and brothers on this earth. The sureness of Rosemary's faith has always given her a sense of harmony and unity in all human experience, and she has vitally enriched our awareness of how being faculty spouse means building collegiality and social inclusiveness in all the Academy family.

Anything but provincial, Rosemary reaches beyond the campus to enrich the town by entering into a multitude of community activities. Her achievements seem endless: starting a hospice in this part of New Hampshire; being president of the PTA and being in the Exeter Players in the 50's; teaching a child to garden; being a model of leadership in the Christ Church Vestry and its Altar Guild; constantly entertaining families at her and David's wonderful table and remembering birthdays from the youngest of us to the eldest; tirelessly dedicating herself to the Exeter Hospital and to Child and Family Services; coaching boys, before coeducation, to walk a light step in dramatic productions; later coaching them in earnest to deal with their fears and their consciences in the 60's and in the early 70's when she worked with them as a draft counselor.

Rosemary works just as indefatigably behind the scenes of public prominence. Those closest to her say that she is, most of all, a good friend. She does prove the maxim, "If you want a job done, give it to the busiest person;" but she proves as well that her life with David is a stunning example of how two busy and highly responsible people can daily cherish *private* joy. She and David so obviously share delight in balancing energy and composure; their example of living in retirement is as successful as their years *in mediis rebus*. They represent an era that has come and, perhaps, gone—an era of professional distinction and of social warmth remarkably mingled. "We are all prouder of our own lives," one of Rosemary's close friends said recently, "because of Rosemary's achievement."

Rosemary was well named Honor. We honor her today, just as she was honored in 1987 by Notre Dame College with a Doctor of Humane

Letters; in 1985 by Concord Academy with the Distinguished Service Award; and in 1982 by the National Association of Social Workers with New Hampshire's Volunteer of the Year. But what is most significant is that Rosemary herself is Honor: honest in word, fair in judgment, principled in action. These distinguished qualities make her the lodestar of those unspoken, but institutionally assumed, achievements of what was once called a faculty wife. In the nomination for this award, it is observed that "Rosemary Coffin was an exemplary faculty wife. She was the last of that breed of wives who devoted their lives to the dormitory and its students. She fed them, cared for them, still keeps in touch with them. By honoring her, the Academy honors every other wife who served the school in that capacity."

Rosemary's active involvement in life began a long time ago. Excerpts from the following article written by a faculty wife is found in *The Grapevine* in 1985. It shows her dedication to the world around her.

A Portrait of Rosemary Coffin
by Amy Lamotte

With an English mother and American father, Rosemary had spent much of her childhood in England, but attended Concord Academy in Massachusetts for twelve years.

...After one year at Radcliffe, she returned to England to join the war effort working at a British-American radio research lab as secretary for a group of scientists who developed radar detection equipment. After the war she went to work at an electrical engineering library in Boston at the request of some of the American scientists...From there she went to New York to work for the Radio Division of the United Nations. There she helped prepare the nightly news broadcasts. "That was fascinating. In 1948, with Israel forming, the meetings got very exciting."

...In the fall of 1948 she returned to England, intending to stay there for good. She worked at the library of Cambridge University's Department of Applied Economics...In the spring of 1949, she met

David who was studying then at Cambridge. They were married in the fall.

...When Rosemary first came to Exeter with David in 1953...Sarah was just under two and Peter was only six weeks old. "That first year was very difficult because the dorm was arranged then so that there was no room where I could get away from the noise. That was a problem for a mother trying to grab moments of sleep during the day. I used to tell the boys who had the room over us that we could hear every word they said, which kept things down to a dull roar."

Rosemary explained that it was her husband who first got her involved with the students by giving her his advisee folders to read. "I looked through them and found when their birthdays were; I found which ones were musical and might want to come in and play the piano, which ones came from split homes, and which ones were on scholarship." She soon found herself complementing David's role as teacher by serving as a friend and confidant, and occasionally as a mother, for the students. She went to see them when they played in a football or baseball game, were in a debate, or gave a recital. She created a large garden and used the flowers she grew to decorate the entrance hall of the dorm. "Quite often when I was out gardening, boys would stop to discuss the flowers, but sometimes they would tell me that they had been writing poetry and would I like to hear some." Sunday afternoons she and David held "open house" when they served dinner to a group of students. She did the make-up for the student plays and helped make their costumes.

...She expressed her strong feelings about how faculty wives can be made to feel more a part of the school in an interview. She felt there was a strong need for teamwork between husband and wife. It works best if the husband lets his wife know enough about his job to make her feel included. Wives find themselves surrounded by young men, and that can be intimidating and frightening if she is not happy in her situation....Rosemary felt that couples without children or few children should not be penalized by being kept on higher floors and in smaller apartments just because of family size. Seniority would allow them to move after a reasonable time in the dorm.

Rosemary would like to see the wife introduced to the campus when the husband is being interviewed. The wife should meet the whole department. When Rosemary and David came to campus, Salty took Rosemary to the grill for coffee. He made her feel involved.

The wife should have some sort of introduction or preparation for dorm life, especially if she had not lived in dorm before. She felt her role earned part of David's income because she contributed. One of many helpful suggestions from Rosemary: hire a house mother for a dorm with a single faculty woman in charge so there is someone to give her time off and help her take off some of the pressure.

Rosemary frequently brought together a group of wives, old and new, to help new wives.

Lack of privacy was a frequent lament as well as a lack of time for the faculty husband to be with his own children. And it was hard to consider the dorm as a "home of one's own."

**Shirley and Bob Brownell
Recipients of Founder's Day Award 1999**

Robert and Shirley Brownell—As a couple, and as individuals, you exemplify Exeter's most cherished ideals: achievement through hard work, service to others, and an unflagging standard of excellence in all things. For 30 years you led, nurtured, and enriched the Academy community, and we honor your inspirational legacy today…

Shirley, you were Bob's partner and teammate in service to Exeter, and you also enriched the Academy community in your own right, particularly for students in Dunbar, Cilley, and Ewald dorms. You were a crucial female role model, especially in the days before coeducation, and later for the first classes of female students. With Bob and your children, Susan, Elizabeth, class of 1971, Martha, class of 1973, and Robert, class of 1979, you created a strong and loving family, then welcomed Exeter students into that family to learn the meaning of devotion, discipline, and fun.

Bob and Shirley, we honor you both for your strong convictions, your dedication to students and to the field of education, and for the broad range of talents you placed in Exeter's service for so many years. We are proud to present you with this 1999 Founder's Day Award.

Shirley's Response to the Award

Our Exeter Career began over forty years ago, in 1958 even before Alaska and Hawaii were states...Founder's Day gives me the perfect opportunity to put on my rose colored glasses and remember those early years at Exeter. We arrived at this all-male bastion with three young daughters while son Bobby arrived a few years later. Bob has taught under five principals, the last being Kendra O'Donnell. Ty, we're sorry we missed you. Bill Saltonstall was our first Principal and the Harkness Teachers were in their prime those early years. The new young teachers as well as students were in awe of them...We spent seventeen years in boys' dorms before moving off campus just as coeducation was getting into full swing.

Dividing our responsibilities was certainly easy for us in those early years. The men taught, coached, ran the dormitories, and advised boys. We wives were their support group. Our major responsibility was family and we enjoyed our role. There were lots of us here. Most like us, had large families and best of all we were in the same boat. The wives were a very close group and our children were just as close. Exeter turned out to be the perfect place to raise our family, even with our three young daughters. Best of all, the action was right here. Friends and playmates were just outside the door; schools and town were within walking distance (Our children never used a school bus.)

The gym, tennis courts and playing fields were just across the street. The children learned to skate on an outdoor rink near the boiler plant.

(This was before the Zamboni when the players had to sweep the ice between periods.) I don't think we ever had to teach the children the rules of any sport. These were also the years of the FBI (Fac Brats Inc.) and the Once-In-A-While Gazette, a Fac Brat newspaper published by the Heath boys. Because his Dad coached basketball, Bobby spent a lot of his early career under the bleachers in Thompson gym and in retaliation he became a hockey player. Susan tells me that Spud was a favorite neighborhood game and I can well remember the endless games of Four Square outside the Dunbar Dining Hall when the Academy boys would include the children who could more than hold their own. No, I never had to be a Soccer Mom. By the time Bobby was ready for kindergarten, I went right along with him and taught there for eleven years.

Bob and I have often wished that our daughters could have enjoyed coeducation as it is today. They would have loved it. Our oldest two, Susan and Beth, went to Northfield, Beth returning to Exeter for her senior year that first year of coeducation. As a matter of fact, she received the first Exeter diploma awarded to a girl. Martha graduated in 1973. Exeter provided Bobby the best of two worlds; he got an Exeter education while living at home.

Our generation referred to the Academy as Uncle Phil. I hope that it still is. Uncle Phil was very kind to the Brownell family. I'm sure that, down the road, you will think back and find that Uncle Phil was a very important member of your family too.

Barbara L. James
Recipient of Founder's Day Award 2002

Barbara L. James—for three decades you raised the political consciousness of this community and so many others. So universally open and caring are you that, over the years, your vocation and personal life have been entwined—the one indistinguishable from the other and both an inspiration.

With Bud, your partner in life and work, you came to Exeter in 1972, bringing with you years of experience as activists. During the peak of the Civil Rights Movement, you had participated in the March to Montgomery as coordinators of the Denver contingent. Activism and a selfless concern for the disenfranchised and downtrodden would remain hallmarks of your work throughout the coming years.

As dorm parents in Wentworth, you and Bud opened your home to dormitory residents and to members of the many clubs you supervised. Together you taught, counseled, fed, inspired and loved these students, and their abiding fondness and respect for you continues to be evident in the numerous alumni/ae who write and call and visit you when they are in the area.

Even in your early years at Exeter, you strove to make a difference in this community, involving yourself in important student and committee work. At a time when faculty spouses and Academy women in general had little to say and even less influence, you and others formed a women's group (P.E.A.Women) at Exeter—for the first time pushing gender equity to the forefront.

Over the years, while staying attuned to social and political issues on campus and beyond, you became more and more immersed in student activities and services. In fact, it was your insight and persistence that encouraged the Exeter community to begin to see and value student activities as a central, rather than a peripheral, component of how we work with young people, and it was because of *your* energy and initiative that the first student center was created at the Academy.

Sociopolitical issues struck a chord with you, and to these you devoted much time and special attention, working indefatigably with Exeter students, public high school students, townspeople, and whomever else you could convince to spread knowledge, find solutions and make a difference. You took an especially strong interest in race relations, homelessness, nuclear energy and its impact, the relationship between developed and developing countries, and local and national politics. Through your own activism and advocacy, you taught Exeter students to translate information and opinions into action—to organize people and rally them around the matter at hand.

You always saw the Academy in the context of its global position, albeit in a small, New England town, and you wanted Exeter students to understand that they attended school in a community where people have jobs and homes and send their children to the other high school down the street. In typical fashion, you developed volunteer programs and fund-raisers, such as the Homeless Vigil, to help the two communities work together to recognize their common ground and respect their differences.

You exemplified and continue to exemplify the dignity of teaching outside the classroom, reminding us that we are all ultimately educators of the students in our charge, whether we are custodians or coaches or instructors. Your unceasing and infectious energy, your rare ability to speak to the conscience of an individual in a loving way, and your passionate example of commitment to the issues that affect our communities and our world, have encouraged a generation of students to pursue work that is meaningful, work that is needed. As a favorite quote of yours from the *Talmud* goes, "It is not incumbent upon thee to complete the task, but neither art thou free to desist from thy part in it." Barbara, for making so many of us feel valued and heard and for never desisting in your pursuit of a better, more equitable life for your fellow human beings, we honor you today with this Founder's Day Award.

Excerpts from Barbara's Response

John Lennon was right, "Life is what happens while you are making other plans."

I'm not sure if I believe in Kismet but while Bud and I were living in Denver, Colorado, I came across a quotation by William B. Saltonstall, Peace Corps Worker in Nigeria, from a writing by the founder of Phillips Exeter Academy during the American Revolution. I'm sure you are all familiar with it.

> "Goodness without knowledge is weak and feeble, yet knowledge without goodness is dangerous. Both united form the noblest character and lay the surest foundation of usefulness to mankind."

We didn't have a clue as to what or where Exeter was but I was totally captivated by this profound message, so I typed it on an index card in "red" and stuck it on my refrigerator. I seriously embraced that ideal. Little did we know that we would end up at Exeter...

We came to Exeter so Bud could teach art and for over a year we just enjoyed academic sanity and our three sons. It wasn't long, however, before a group of spouses, staff and some faculty women formed the dorm life study group which encouraged the administration to employ counselors and establish three day weekends...

A best day at Exeter was being able to help a student realize her potential and stay at the academy. We will never forget the day when the boys in Williams House had constructed a thousand paper cranes for their dorm head, Bette Ogami, who had been stricken with a life consuming cancer. Then there was some time to sit in the swing under the beautiful copper beech tree in front of the library...

We really know that there is much to do, which brings me to my most passionate interest: an Exeter where Community Service has been expanded to become a part of the culture, an integral part of the curriculum. It need not be a requirement but should be so enticing and rewarding that most of you will want to be part of it. Community Service can be done in a more educated, productive and rewarding manner. It is time to make goodness a full partner with knowledge...

You are often referred to as the "Best and the Brightest." I'm sure you are bright or you wouldn't be here, but the best? We all have our whole life to become the best and even then there will always be multitudes who are better. But we do have each and every day to do our best.

I hope you accept that I truly believe you are amazing. You do have the power to change the world and the power to make sure it doesn't change you...

Chapter 14

Principals' Wives

From the very beginning, the principal's wife had a tough assignment. She had no "job description" but was ready to entertain students, faculty, trustees and visitors. She hosted overnight guests, welcomed new faculty wives by having teas and by visiting them in their homes. She even did dorm duty in the girls' dorms to be closer to the pulse of the school while continuing her professional interests.

Rosemary Coffin in "Garland of Phillipa" describes the activities of the Principal's wife this way:

> [Phillipa] marveled at Eleanor's ability to cope with the Principal's house, her four children, the constant demands to entertain parents, faculty, students, and the Trustees on their quarterly meetings. On top of that how did she find time to garden and visit wives who were new or sick or troubled? She seemed to have a sixth sense with the last. It wasn't just faculty wives who felt her concern; it was also the wives of men who worked on maintenance, and the women who worked in the dining hall. (page 44)

Principals' Wives

(Years the Principal was in office)
1783-1788

Elizabeth Brooks

m. William Woodbridge
Daughter of Deacon Brooks, resident on Front St. She died in childbirth, 1787, leaving one daughter.

1788-1838

| Hannah Tracy Emery | m. Benjamin <u>Abbot</u> She died in 1793, leaving one son |
| Mary Perkins | (second wife) three children, one died. |

Of Boston, a woman of strong and beautiful character. On account of her high social position many of the villagers at first looked askance at her, and assumed that she would "put on airs." But Mrs. A mingled freely among people of all classes, and concerned herself so sincerely with bettering the condition of the poor it was not many weeks before she was loved by everyone. Her unfeigned goodness could neither be resisted nor denied.[5]

The Abbots lived in the old John Phillips Mansion on Water Street from 1798-1811 when the new house for the Principal was built on open land near the Academy building (across the street from the present Academy Building) where they lived until he died in 1849. "Moving from the house on fashionable Water Street, in the heart of the community life, was so severe a wrench that Mrs. Abbot shed tears of regret. The new house stood 'in the sands,' almost in the country from the little village,...both the house and the surroundings were exceedingly "raw."[6]

Mary survived Benjamin for many years, "a cherished remembrance of the past."[7] She died in 1863 at 93 years.

---

5 Cunningham, p35.

6 Myron R. Williams, *The Story of Phillips Exeter, 1781-1956,* Phillips Exeter Academy, Exeter, NH ©1957, p67.

7 Cunningham, p35.

1838-1873
Elizabeth Phillips Emery

m.Gideon Lane <u>Soule</u> in 1822. Five children

1873-1883
Caroline Cleveland

m. Albert C. <u>Perkins</u>, three daughters, one son

1884-1889
wife
[No references found]

m. Walter Q. <u>Scott</u>

1890-1895
Mellie Rowe

m. Charles Everett <u>Fish</u> in 1878. She was his student in Auburn, Maine

1895-1913
Mary Browne Rawson

m. Harlan Page <u>Amen</u>.
three daughters, Margaret, Elizabeth, Perne, and son, John.

Mary Browne Rawson "was a woman of rare tact and beauty of character whose influence over her husband was great."[8]

They had no home when they arrived. Carpenters were working on the Principal's House at Abbot Place. Trustee Wm. P Chadwick who lived on Front Street (in a house where the Inn at Exeter is now) took them in for three weeks. She died in 1901.

---

8 Laurence M. Crosbie, *The Phillips Exeter Academy, A History*, The Plimpton Press, Norwood MA, ©1924, p179.

<u>1914-1946</u>

Margaret L. Hubbell
m. Lewis <u>Perry</u>. Margaret died in 1928, leaving children Lewis and Emily.

Unlike the other faculty wives Margaret "brought a sense of world outside Exeter. Her informality of dress and manner baffled as much as it delighted...The Academy will never know how much it owes to Margaret Perry and how much it lost in her untimely death from breast cancer in 1928.[9]

Juliette Adams (sister of his first wife, Margaret) married Lewis in 1935

<u>1947-1963</u>

Katharyn Watson
m. William Gurdon <u>Saltonstall</u> in 1931.

five children: Josephine, Katharyn, William Jr., Samuel and Deborah.

(See Founder's Day Awards)

<u>1963-1964</u>

Jan Wicks
m. Ernie <u>Gillespie</u> Latin teacher 1939-63, interim Principal 1963-1964

<u>1964-1974</u>

Kathy MacAusland
m. Richard <u>Day.</u> three children Lydia, Andy and Ward

"Having worked closely with Kathy this year on both *The Grapevine* and the Sounding Board, we have come to know

---

9 Williams, p103.

and appreciate the contributions that she has made in many areas of Academy life. In the 10 years that she has been here, Kathy has been instrumental in developing avenues of communication that have created better understanding and a more positive atmosphere.

One of Kathy's first projects was to gather faculty wives at 27 Pine Street for informal luncheons (the baggie lunch era). Over the years this developed into an organization known as the Sounding Board, which represents the interests of women on campus. Another of Kathy's interests was the formation of a newsletter that would be a vehicle of communication for faculty families. This is *The Grapevine*.

In addition to her many other contributions, Kathy is leaving us these two important and ongoing legacies. We thank her and wish her well."

The Grapevine May 1974

1974-1986
Jeanne Godolphin   m. Steve <u>Kurtz</u>

From Jeanne's response to questionnaire:

I did know what boarding school was like because I went to Dana Hall for two years and we were at Kent School for four years. We were married twenty-five years approximately when we came to Exeter.

Exeter was much bigger than Kent so I knew it would be different and very different in that Steve came as Principal.

I wanted to support Steve but certainly wanted my own life as well. We entertained students in our home—big groups, little groups, all ways. I taught at UNH and for two years, was a Teaching Assistant at Boston University. I was on the boards of social services agency in town.

I basically have very good memories of the 14 years we spent at Exeter. I tried to support faculty wives, as well as Emeriti wives, and felt in turn that they really supported me. A good number turned out to be warm and loving friends. I particularly appreciated the fact that I never really felt criticism of my studying and working at another institution. As far as I was concerned this just enriched my own relationships at the

Academy. (At times it felt like a lot of work, trying to be a good Principal's wife and having my own career, but I chose it and I liked it!)

As for students...they were the ones who made it all feel so very worthwhile. I was fortunate enough to personally get to know a good number quite well and that felt really good. I loved the fact that they were all so different and it is this which, to my mind, differentiates Exeter from the other prep schools I had known.

1986-1997
Patrick O'Donnell   m. Kendra O'Donnell

1997-
Marcia Morgenstern   m. Tyler Tingley

When Marcia and Ty came to Exeter they had been married for twenty-nine years and had two sons, Chase, who was at Harvard, and Morgan, who entered the Academy as an Upper. Marcia offers this:

> From the beginning, Ty described our relationship as a partnership. For the first few years, when he would give a short speech at the opening faculty party, I would add a few words as well; and I have spoken at all the alumni/ae gatherings up until this year, (2002) when the format of the Saturday morning "conversation with the Principal" changed.
>
> We have always felt that entertaining was an important part of our lives. The first year we were here, we invited every member of the PEA community—faculty, staff, and students—to our home over the course of the year, in addition to hosting trustee, alumni/ae, and parent events. We have not continued at quite the same pace in subsequent years, but we do invite every faculty member (and spouse or partner) to at least one event during the year, as well as many staff members. We also have all the students here, either for a "dorm study break" or for "afternoon tea." We have had between thirty and fifty events at Saltonstall House each year, as well as hosting another twenty-five or more at other venues.
>
> As my professional work life has been entirely in the computer arena, I have been a member of the Academic and

Administrative Technology Committees, which are looking at how technology should be used at the Academy both near-term and in the future. I was also a member of the faculty-staff same-sex housing study group that discussed the issues the Academy would face in implementing a policy that allowed same-sex partners to live in Academy housing.

Getting to know the students has been one of the best parts of being here. While Morgan was a student, I knew more names and heard more about what was going on every day. However, I've also been a dorm affiliate in McConnell Hall since our first term here, which has given me a way to learn first-hand about daily life at the Academy. I do dorm duty once a week and join the dorm on outings such as Academy Life Day and Environmental Day. I've felt very privileged to be able to become friends with some of the students and to feel that I have been part of their lives for a few years...

The boarding experience in the family was mine, as I had attended Milton for four years as a boarding student. In some ways, things haven't changed too much, although in many other ways, they are very different. Exeter feels like a rare opportunity to live with some of the brightest and most talented high school students in the world, and I feel very fortunate to be a part of it.

Chapter 15

Looking Back

As a dormitory wife for twenty-four years, Helen Stuckey's advice to new wives was "first...people are essentially good, and good-willed. It is one's own inner discipline, *not discipline imposed*, and that makes the man. Any day is the better for doing something for someone else. Secondly...ask interested questions, be as knowledgeable as possible about a boy's activities, and encourage him to talk about himself. Dorm life? Enjoy it! Try to get to know the students, and savor them. Participate in the life of the school—you will enjoy it!"

Dorothy Lloyd, faculty wife from 1931 to 1962, wrote the following Letter to the Editor in *The Grapevine*, October of 1975: "As for the problems—like death and taxes they're always with us, on every level of living—dorm, school, town, state, nation. But every faculty wife learns rather soon that the problems she copes with as a wife, mother, partner with her husband in the dormitory experience are inextricably linked in a chain that leads from family, to dormitory, to the school, to the town, to the state and to the nation....It was exciting to have been a faculty wife. It is still exciting to feel very much a part of Phillips Exeter Academy."

Lucy Weeks' (1935) daughter, Margie, offered this about her mother: "I now know that my mother recognized that Exeter afforded opportunities that she would otherwise not have had, but on the other hand, it was diminishing in ways that may be difficult to explain to a succeeding generation. She found the Academy both stifling and enriching. She often defended the role of faculty wife to younger faculty wives who challenged it, while herself chafing under its limitations."

Libby Bickel (1936) felt "like the academy was a 'mother hen' watching over us, giving us advantages we otherwise would not have had." In her day the faculty stayed for many years, and there was a feeling of

110

a larger family. The only negative was the politics of the housing assignments.

Helen Clark (1937) said: "At no time in our years at the Academy did I feel like a second-class citizen. In Dr. Perry's and Bill Saltonstall's June letters of appreciation to Bill I remember it was always 'Thank you and Helen for all you do for the school.'"

Barbara Little(1939) remains a big fan of Exeter and upholds it as the greatest school in the country.

Mary Stevens (1942) felt quite differently. "Naively the Academy thought wives were of no importance to the school. They existed at the choice of their husbands, to care for children and did or did not associate with the students, a matter of whose choice I never really knew."

Betty Brinckerhoff (1947) had a loyalty to the school, especially where the dorm was concerned. "Yes, there was a lack of privacy, and no feeling of a home of your own, and dorm duty could be demanding twenty-four hours a day, but you couldn't beat the rent. If you came to the boarding school you knew what the situation was, so accept what is there."

For Mary Echols (1957, her memories are of different events:

Watching Robinson Female Seminary burn.

Watching moving of houses from one side of Main Street to the other to become dorms.

Sledding down Tan Lane with the Heyls after snow.

Going to Boston often on Wednesday afternoons to book movies for the boys to be shown in the Gym.

Enjoying visiting lecturers and musicians. Eubie Blake, Robert Frost.

Finding small treasures in trench dug behind Principal's House preparatory to building new Library.

Faculty Christmas Parties in Lamont Gallery.

Enjoying Bicentennial Celebration with Concert of Boston Pops.

Ice skating on the frozen River near the playing fields.

Margot Trout (1961) had a much different feeling abut the school. The longer she stayed at Exeter the more resentful she became at being in an institution where she had no voice. She explains it this way:

At one point the headmaster's wife, Kathy Day, started a lunch group of faculty wives. The topic came up of what a wife should do when she had an idea about the school. It was generally agreed that one persuaded one's husband that it was his idea. I thought this was so disgusting that I resigned from the group.

Faculty wives had a terribly limited role as I saw it centered around their home and dorm lives. Working outside the home was rare. I felt very stifled and was delighted to leave. I remember hearing while I was there that aptitudes are dynamic not inert, and if they are not used they drive you crazy. I learned during that time the truth of this for me.

Right from the beginning Joan Lyford (1963) recognized how ingrown and insular life at the Exeter Academy could be:

Socially we never entertained with just our academy friends but kept our contact with friends from Durham and the art world.

I did not make a big deal about my concerns. I wore protective coloring and bore from within to make what changes I could. I have enormous respect for Kathy Day. Being chosen to her group of change makers (we called ourselves the "Baggies" in honor of our bag lunches; also known as the Sounding Board) was a real eye opener into the ways wives had been grossly overlooked in the past. It was through her that apartments were renovated and an interior decoration policy was established. There were other changes.

Ernie Gillespie's phrasing of Exeter's philosophy, "This is not a warm nest, but when you come back to visit, you will be warmly welcomed," or words to that effect, seemed to permeate the campus for new faculty as well as students. Greetings were not exchanged on campus paths, and invitations to others' homes, with one exception, were not forthcoming for over a year—even for an alumnus returning to teach. Perhaps one explanation might be protection of privacy in close living quarters or New Hampshire reserve, but it was an interesting phenomenon which ended completely when girls arrived on campus.

Later, I tried to make new wives more welcome by showing them some of the town's places of interest.

Anne Rogers (1967) wrote: "After many years of teaching which we
had enjoyed, our years at PEA seemed like whipped cream on top of
the pudding."

When Charlie and Betty Terry (1967) lived in the dormitory, they
had a wonderful relationship with his students. "We were an affection-
ate team, and I found it enjoyable and positive to fulfill some of the
obligations. Charlie and I were not 'two for the price of one' since I led
my own life from the beginning of our years here. Many of the students who were my friends in the dormitory are now between their
late twenties and their early fifties, and they are, to this day, among our
best friends."

What Carole Rindfleisch (1968) remembered looking back were benefits and drawbacks:

Benefits of Years at the Academy:

Outstanding, and free education for our four children.

Living in a secure and supportive community with rich cultural
opportunities on campus.

Living in an atmosphere of excitement and enthusiasm about learning.

Delicious and nutritious meals in the Dining Halls.

Sabbatical, personal leaves, School Year Abroad (France);
Opportunities for travel and refreshing change of pace.

Pride in working with wonderful students, especially in the Library,
and in being part of a dedicated Library staff.

Excellent health plan.

Drawbacks:

Difficulty in insulating oneself and the family from student problems.

Lack of privacy not a major issue when we lived on campus but we
really appreciated living off campus after ten years of advisees.

Moving off campus meant that three of our children became day
students which greatly curtailed their previous freedom as on-
campus fac brats.

Barbara Crowe (1968) found Exeter a wonderful place to raise a family:

I enjoyed the camaraderie of other families and the advantages of sharing their lives with us...

Living in a dormitory had its challenges! Some of the kids were wonderful and some, simply hard to be around. Many of them were considered "family," others were interlopers. All of them demanded a great deal of time from my husband and the children's father. The only way to survive in this situation was to become part of it—and we did.

The one problem for me was that we all put so much heart and love into sharing our home with these students that when some would leave at the end of the year(s) without a good-bye or a thank you it was depressing. Of course, most did close the relationship, but often the child you spent the most energies on, left without a good-bye or allowing us the opportunity to meet his family. We discovered over the years that this is no different with college kids!

Corinna Hammond (1973) also thought Exeter a good place for family:

Exeter was a great place to raise a family. The town is great, good public schools and the children could walk to school. But the real plus was being on campus.

The school is like an old-fashioned village—for better or worse everyone knows you and your children. Staff, teachers, administrators, students, they all had an eye on your kids. Best of all, there was always a large pool of other children for your children to play with. And they were always visible; right outside the window (we were in Abbot). I enjoyed the other mothers and the "we're all-in-this-together" camaraderie.

But the key element was the closeness of Davis' and the children's lives. They knew what Davis did and how he spent his time.

"Life" and work were intermingled and it was constant. The children grew up, but their world was steady and nurturing with just enough yearly shake-up to be interesting. We had wonderful facilities, free housing and three meals a day. Hard to beat that.

Nancy Pierce (1971) thoroughly enjoyed her years at PEA. "It was a great place to raise small children. And I was not aware of how insular PEA was until I was Adult Education Director at the Exeter High School. Around 1987 a faculty member (female) had signed up for an Adult Education course and did not know where Exeter High School was! Unfortunately I suspect I was very oblivious to many town happenings when we were at PEA."

Carol Hamblet (1979) remembers:
Feeling exhausted.
Wonderful friends and student relationships.
Parents with similar values in raising children.
Having your children as Exeter students is when you find out what
   is *really* happening in the classroom.

Carol Tucker's (1980) years at the Academy were good years with wonderful friendships.

Women and children were together often because of the many functions our spouses attended. Our children grew up together in the luxury of good food, safe play areas, the pool, the playing fields, the endless source of activity, the Quad.

There were so many wonderful lingering walks with friends to and from the dining hall, times to sit and talk with friends because of our mutual bond—"The Exeter Community," a place for us to thrive in. Never since have our two sons, Dylan and Ross, felt as accepted and welcomed as when we lived at PEA.

An appreciation for the wives' support of the students and for what wives gave to the school was expressed by a former student:

A noted alumnus died at the same time as Edith Leonard, a faculty wife who lived in the dorm for twenty-five years. The academy flag had not been lowered for an alumnus before, and the student was incensed that the flag was flown at half mast for the alum and not for a faculty wife.

Conclusions

Living in a secondary boarding school had it rewards and challenges. The wives who spoke of their lives at the Phillips Exeter Academy spoke honestly about what was positive about the school, and what made it difficult. Each brought her own abilities and outlook on life to the new assignment. Life as a house mother in a mansion of 40 to 60 rooms inhabited with adolescent boys high on life was not a scene necessarily familiar to the wives who walked onto campus for the first time. The adjustment to this new life was shaped in part by each individual's ability to make the best of a new reality, and to shape that reality into a meaningful life.

All of the wives had thoughts about how to help new wives see the potential for richness and challenges in the academic environment. The interview was the first contact with the school, and offered an opportunity to make the candidate's wife feel included and part of the encompassing totality of her husband's job. If she met all of the members of the department and their wives, toured the campus, saw students on the paths, even met some, she had a much better idea of what this environment was, how exciting and busy it could be. One wife went to the Grill with the Principal, another joined her husband for dinner with the department faculty and their wives.

The Founder's Day Award given to Rosemary Coffin states: "You show how a faculty spouse means building collegiality and social inclusiveness in all the Academy faculty." This would include not only the students, but staff and other faculty. The school is a community, and how we share our lives with all others enriches not only our lives but the life of the school as a whole. Teas and coffees for new wives and visits from other wives helped to bring the newest wife into the community.

Many of the wives felt that, by being a part of a team with their husbands, they helped to improve the dorm atmosphere as well as afford her husband more time with the family. If a wife read about the students, she could pick up information about birth dates for parties, a student from a broken home, or someone with a special talent. She would know their names, interact with them in the dorm, might check them in, unlock doors, and attend their games, concerts and plays. The wives who shared in the dormitory routine expressed their feeling that they felt more a part of the school, and were happier because of it.

The women who had previous experience in a boarding school, either as a student or faculty wife, found it easy to enter into school life. Also, women who were in their late twenties or older and new to the boarding school environment seemed to adjust more easily than the younger women.

The words offered for Barbara James in her Founder's Day Award speak to all of us: "You exemplified and continue to exemplify the dignity of teaching outside the classroom, reminding us that we are all ultimately educators of the students in our charge, whether we are custodians or coaches or instructors." Or faculty spouses.

The faculty wife has an important job, one to which she brings her own special talents, abilities and personality. She teaches by example, by how she works with her husband and interacts with her family in the dormitory, on the paths and in the dining hall, and by what she does with her talent or gift as a volunteer or a professional. How she shares her lives with the students teaches the "goodness" complement to "knowledge."

Part III

Daughters

Chapter 16

Before Coeducation

The years before and during the early Harkness years were idyllic for Charlotte Cushwa Clark and her close friend Lucy Hulburd Richardson. Charlotte Cushwa was the daughter of English teacher Frank William Cushwa, Academy faculty from 1907 to 1939, and his wife, Elizabeth Tucker, daughter of President Tucker of Dartmouth College. Charlotte Clark responded to the request for women's' stories and memories in the Spring 2000 issue of the Exeter Bulletin with the following letter:

August 21, 2000

Dear Mrs. Brown,

...I grew up at Exeter as the daughter of a faculty member and have a son, William Tucker Clark, who graduated in 1963 from Exeter. I would like to add a few of my own memories of life at Exeter as a child.

My name is Charlotte Cushwa Clark (Mrs. Bayard Stockton Clark) and I was born in 1917 at the Exeter hospital. My brother, William Tucker Cushwa (Bill), followed in 1918 and we lived in a wonderful Victorian house, called Ed Gilman (now apartments, called the Cushwa House.) Our home faced Court Street and had a long sloping lawn, a barn and a porte-cochere. We were dislodged for a year when the house was moved to make room for Wentworth Hall (where my life long friend and faculty daughter, Lucy Richardson lived), Amen Hall, and Cilley Hall (where another life long friend, Lucy Williams Quimby, lived.) Later, Dean Kerr would call us the Three Graces. Ed Gilman House was moved to Elm Street with less spacious grounds where my father, Frank William Cushwa, who was an avid gardener, planted gardens. We ate at Dunbar Hall dining room at the faculty table. Lucy Quimby and I were the only two girls and we enjoyed it thoroughly! I was eventually sent to boarding school at Dana Hall leaving the Robinson Female Seminary. I did not get annoyed that I could not go to Exeter until the feminist movement caught up with me!

I loved growing up in Exeter. It was like a large extended family. I have many memories of going to Exeter-Andover games, canoeing on the Exeter River, and going to Sunday chapel services. One interesting memory was the graduation ceremony of General Pershing's son [1927]. I was just old enough to appreciate the excitement and the wonderful fruit-shaped ice sherbet!

Now my desire is to retrieve my father's portrait from the archives and have it put in the Cushwa room in the old library.

I am happy to write this letter and am sincerely yours,

Charlotte C. Clark."

[Frank Cushwa's Portrait was dedicated March of 2002 in the Elting Room in Phillips Hall.]

Potpourri

Charlotte, and her family lived with twelve students on Court Street in the house which became Cushwa House on Elm Street. Her father's study was the sun room at the back of the house. He was a gardener and had a peony bed beside the house. Her father was instrumental in the founding of the art department of the Academy, along with Tom Folds.

Ethel Doe, whose father was a math teacher at the Academy, was Charlotte's "big sister" at Robinson Female Seminary. Ice skating on the river afforded them the opportunity to meet with the daughters of the Polish mill workers.

There were boardwalks between the buildings on campus because the yard was very wet. The girls would look for coins under the walkways.

During the Depression they lived in an "ivory tower." Only the sons of wealthy parents, such as Baccarat and Neiman Marcus, could afford to come. Her family sponsored a wealthy Japanese student during this time.

Famous people were a part of her life. Her family had a party for Robert Frost when he came to campus. Carl Sandburg also came to campus. One of the students in their house was Richard Bissell, author of *The Pajama Game.*

Miss Smith's School on Court Street was attended by many faculty children. The school was one classroom, grades 1,2, and 3, with about 20 students. The house was two houses down from the Court Street School. Charlotte's memories of her life as a faculty daughter are fond memories.

Lucy Hulburd Richardson was born to Phillip Hulburd, mathematics teacher, and his wife Gladys Elizabeth Heywood Hulburd. They came to the Academy in 1919, and her father remained on the faculty until 1959. The family lived in Wentworth Hall during the war years, filling in for a bachelor who had gone to serve in the forces. They then moved to Moulton House where they were the first occupants after the Academy purchased the property in 1945.

Lucy remembers the Seminary Pond on the Lincoln Street corner of the Seminary property. Here they would play and collect polliwogs. The area was later filled in.

Mrs. Merrill had a large garden behind her home, (now Merrill House dormitory) where Fisher Theater stands. "The secret garden was along a small stream with a little bridge that humped up in the middle quite steeply. She had a large flower and vegetable garden between her house and the Dow House next door, unlike anything else in the neighborhood."

In 1925 large blocks of ice were delivered to the dorm for their "ice box." This was in the days before refrigeration. And there was the Old Grill behind Peabody Hall.

Seward's Drugstore on Water Street was perfect for ice-cream cones dipped in chocolate sprills. And London's Dry Goods was a favorite for after school-adventures.

Square dancing became a popular Saturday evening entertainment. At first they met in Gilman House when the Littles lived there. Later they danced in the dining room of Langdell Hall during vacations.

Lucy remembers skating on the "fresh river all the way out to the foot of Shaw's Hill where we would study the patterns of the grasses locked in the ice over the flooded meadows. When there was snow and we were not skating, we skied over the Hill Bridge along the fields behind the High Street houses to a respectable slope on which we practiced for the bigger and higher slopes on Moulton's Ridge, and later on, at Jackson, New Hampshire, or Woodstock, Vermont."

Lucy and her two friends, Lucy Quimby and Charlotte Cushwa, attended Robinson Female Seminary until they went away to boarding schools to finish their high school education. Lucy also remembers the graduation reception where the sherbet ice was shaped like fruits.

Lucy found that there was always plenty to do with the friends she grew up with at the Academy. They were always happy, and felt privileged to have been a part of campus life.

Home

In the early 20th century the Academy was an all-male environment. The first families to live on campus had to persuade some of the men to accept the idea of family and of women on campus. It was not always comfortable for the girls, their mothers or the new faculty member. For example, when her family lived in Abbot Hall, Edith Leonard Greene's her mother put out a pole clothes hanger with diapers on it. There was a terrific "to-do" in faculty meeting, which Edith's parents took fairly hard.

The issue of laundry was solved by confining the drying of clothes to the steam room, therefore maintaining the academic appearance of the campus. It took time, but eventually the atmosphere began to be more accepting of families.

Emily Perry's Birthday Party, June 1927. Jane Anne Fiske, Virginia Pearson, Roma Leacock, Ann Cary Stuckey, Dan Stuckey, Lucy Hulburd, Lewis Perry Jr., Lynn Kirtland, Bobby Hulburd, Harlan Robinson, George Richardson, Margaret Fiske Plazier and daughter, Mary, Judith Fiske, Emily Perry, Mrs. Margaret Perry, Ann Richardson, Mrs. Davis Shute, Henry W. Shute and Alfred Wightman.

(Photo courtesy of Judith Fiske Gross)

Though children knew they should be seen and not heard, especially around the classroom buildings, the rest of the campus belonged to them. When the girls were young, memories of campus as personal playground are many. As they became teenagers, the loss of privacy or discomfort with the attention from the boys creeps into their narratives.

Anne Leonard Whitney (1947) remembers:

As a young child (pre-teens) I found living at the Academy perfectly fine. The grounds and campus were like a park: large, grassy areas with bushes for games; paved sidewalks for biking, roller-skating, riding in wagons; empty classroom buildings on Wednesday afternoons and weekends for exploring and drawing on blackboards. Lee Taylor and his yard helpers let me rake and "work" with them. During winter and spring vacations we could play in the empty dorms. The dining rooms and kitchen in Merrill and Langdell were really special places, with an electric dumb-waiter we could ride in. The students were friendly and the other faculty were like an extended family of aunts and uncles.

Elizabeth Rhoades Aykroyd (1962) "had the whole campus to play in. There were 'houses' behind the forsythia at Hoyt, 'store counters' at the 1910 gate by Peabody, a sledding hill behind Abbot, and the walks were wonderful for roller-skating. The outdoor rink was there for skating. We never went in a building, although during vacations we could play in the corridors of our own dorms."

Julie Rindfleisch Granville (1977) describes how it felt to have the campus as her personal backyard:

> Instead of an ordinary backyard to play in, we had an entire campus to explore—marble statues and stairways to climb on, bushes to hide inside, long dormitory hallways to slide down during the winter vacation. And when you got tired of your brothers and sisters, there was always someone else to play with. Often there were enough other kids around to get some really good games going. We rode our bikes everywhere, with a remarkable degree of freedom...The resultant freedom was great and instilled a spirit of independence and exploration in all of us. The playing fields that stretch out to the banks of the Exeter River held a special attraction, as did the footbridge which led to the three black cannons and the infamous *A Separate Peace* rope swing.

The larger apartments had room for not only the immediate family, but relatives as well. One daughter felt her dorm apartment was like home where there was always room for relatives to stay with them. "We always had a guest room, occupied at various times by elderly relatives (great aunts). This was fairly common at the time, I think. There were grandmothers in the Thomas, Rickard and Phillips households, for instance. From what I've seen since leaving Exeter, the space for a relative was a precious and unusual benefit in a boarding school."

The Yards were their playground, but the dormitories were their homes where privacy was an issue for some. Dormitory life was almost all the daughters knew as home. There may have been things that irked, but on the whole it was a grand place to live. Privacy for the girls may have been less an issue than for their mothers, but the intrusion of the students into their home lives could be troublesome. Marilyn Easton discovered that sounds carried outside the apartment. "Dorm privacy was not an issue until I was learning piano and one of the boys mentioned he could hear me practice. The student said to father, 'Marilyn is getting better.' I was mortified. I never wanted to practice after that."

When the boys came to see Edith Leonard Greene's (1944) father in the dorm apartment, they would sometimes turn the wrong way, and end up in the Leonards' living room where the girls might be in their pajamas.

For birthdays, Miss Gillis, who was in charge of the dining hall, made cake, and it was served at the table during the dinner. When Tootie Wilson Cole (1947) was a teenager, the boys had their eyes on her. One day a student got up from his table and brought just Tootie a piece of his birthday cake. Whereupon, Tootie got up, went over and thanked him. The boys got all flustered, shifting in their seats, unsure as to whether they should stand for a lady.

Marion Wilson Chandler (1949) and her siblings had bedrooms on the 3rd floor of Dunbar. The door connecting their hallway with the hallway of the dorm had a transom above it which could be opened only from the boys' side. Occasionally, as a prank, the students would open it.

Ellen Clark Peck (1961) came home from a date to find the windows in the dorm lined with her "brothers."

The arrangement of the Merrill Hall dining room made dining hall experience more tolerable for Elizabeth Rhoades Aykroyd (1962) than for some. "The door from the corridor to the dining hall table was close by our table so I could slip in and out unobtrusively."

As in the general culture before 1970, most mothers were home with their families. This meant that for the faculty children there were endless homes to go to with many "aunts and uncles" and other children to play with all over a campus that was their own private backyard.

Education

The Robinson Female Seminary (RFS) was the only school in town for high-school-age girls until 1956 when the boys' school, Tuck, was combined with RFS to form the co-ed Exeter High School. The RFS education was adequate, but not up to a rigorous standard, which caused discontent among some of the parents as well as their daughters. Some daughters attended the RFS, while others went to girls' private schools for some or all of their high school education. For the girls who wanted to attend a class at the Academy regular session or Summer School, at first there was strong opposition.

Though Edith Leonard Greene (1944) accepted the fact that girls could not attend the Academy, one incident rankled. "I always wanted to attend one class that my father taught, but was never able to. As the years went by, I resented increasingly my not being able to attend both the school and my father's class."

Margaret Hogg Upham's (1944) parents always made certain her homework was done.

> Many an evening I spent in my father's study doing math, which was not my strong point. Before I went on to college, my father decided that I should take his summer school chemistry course. I had had a year of chemistry at Walnut Hill and the school used his textbook, which was written by him in conjunction with Charlie Bickel. He, of course, had to get permission to allow me in his classroom but he prevailed, and it was a stimulating experience as I sailed through organic and inorganic chemistry in college. He was a wonderful teacher.

For Margaret Clarkson Schoene (1953) "life in Exeter in the early 1950's was stimulating and challenging but also intimidating. I would have loved to attend art classes at the Academy."

Marilyn Easton (1958) did not question that the Academy was for boys only. She didn't resent it; times were just different. Now she wishes she could have stayed at the Academy as she was very homesick at boarding school. Her father, Howard, the coach of the Rifle Club, which was established to prepare boys to go to war, allowed Marilyn to use the range along with the boys when he was there. On the other hand, she was not allowed to attend her father's Latin class in Summer School.

Elizabeth Rhoades Aykroyd (1962) took a typing class at PEA which met at 4:30 in the afternoon. "We paid a fee for me to attend, but I was required to be escorted to class past all those teen boys. As it was they rushed past, too anxious to get to their next class to pay me any attention."

Going to Exeter as a faculty daughter did not interest Sarah Coffin O'Connor (1969). "I was relieved to go away, to not have a parent-advisor situation. But, at the same time, I would have liked to attend Exeter because of the excellence of the school. As it was, I learned to interact with girls by attending Concord Academy, an all-girl school."

In the late 1960's, just prior to coeducation, Lisa Compton Bellocchio (1971), home from Concord Academy on vacation, was allowed to attend one of her father's science classes. When she attended Summer School she was delighted to finally have a dorm room of her own.

Entertainment

Though daughters did not attend classes before coeducation, they attended the abundance of other activities. The Sunday Evening Lecture Series, the sporting events, movies in town, Exeter Players productions, Gilbert and Sullivan Sunday afternoon teas and square dancing at the Little's. They spoke fondly of the different rinks and the birthday parties on the ice. One daughter still has her red skating skirt. And some girls were fortunate to be invited to school dances.

Night skating at the Marston Lane Rink, c.1954
(Photo courtesy of Academy Archives)

Judith Fiske Gross (1942) remembers a time when she brought friends from Walnut Hill to PEA for a dance.

> It was a very rainy night. Instead of walking to the gym my father drove us in the big black '36 Buick. When the dance was over he came back to get us, and after the four of us had gotten into the car another couple climbed in. Father never said a word, just calmly drove to the Inn and left them off. We never knew who they were or if they knew they had been driven home by a unique taxi service.

> Also, father was in charge of keeping the Academy Clock working properly and kept on time. I remember him standing out on the front steps with his pocket watch in his hand making sure the clock struck noon at the exactly correct moment.

Judy tells of her memories of football games, and the victory celebrations after a successful Andover game are vivid:

> As soon as the bell started to ring we knew that there would be a bonfire and the team drawn through the town in a

wagon pulled by boys in their pajamas. Then speeches and cheers and general rowdiness around the bonfire. All this came to a tragic end when the Orton boy was run over by the wagon and later died. Much later Wells Kerr told me that he had built a big fire in his fireplace and he and the boy's parents had sat up all night and talked. He said that he didn't know what else to do. Sadly, I've had occasions to sit around a fire with parents who have just lost a child and I think it is about all you can do.

Faculty daughters could be mischief makers, even at the highest level. Judith Fiske, best friend of Emily Cox (c.1942), remembers a story about Emily and her father:

I think I am the only one living who knows this story. Sometime when she was a teenager she telephoned her father at his office. She pretended to be an upset mother calling about her son. She mumbled her name and his and kept saying hysterically, "But he's such a sensitive boy!" When he asked her name she would mumble something and shriek, "He's such a sensitive boy!" According to his secretary he was frantically looking through the school list to try to figure out who he was talking to. Finally she hung up and when she got around to admitting to her father that it was she, she said to me, "Father didn't think it was the least bit funny." She and I thought it was hilarious and I still enjoy thinking about it!

I also remember that as a child she had to move out of her room when her father had distinguished guests visiting at One Abbot Place. She had a little bathroom connected to her room, which I think was the reason she was asked to move, because there were plenty of other bedrooms in the house. I remember once that she was quite irritated because James Forrestall, Secretary of Defense, was using her room. The fact that he was a famous person didn't impress her at all.

Joey Saltonstall Dubois (1951) has a fond memory about dancing.

I remember a 'coming of age' kind of thing. I used to love to hang out at the Grill. At first it was just the food and the freedom of stopping in on my own usually after baby-sitting for $.25 an hour. But by 9th grade, I guess this "tomboy" who was usually out climbing trees or playing baseball with Jane Leonard, was suddenly also becoming aware of all those young Academy students. When John Coles—a senior yet— who was either editor of *The Exonian* or head of student government, asked me to go to the Spring Dance, I was floored. I also accepted! Neither of us was anything special to the other (probably his girlfriend couldn't come), but what the heck. If the senior I "idolized" wouldn't ask me, all of a sudden that dance became the place I most wanted to be.

I had a wonderful time. I literally felt like all my sensibilities and preferences were affected. *Overnight* I had become a young woman. Later, of course, being invited to the June Ball became of prime interest, and who should arrange that but the senior I idolized, Corky Ellis, whose younger brother Bill agreed to take me.

When the ballet or opera companies came to Boston Nancy Bissell Goldcamp (1959) got out of school for a day and she and her mother, Sally, would go in on the train. In addition, Nancy also "loved the concerts on campus. What a joy to have such excellent musicians from the music faculty and visitors like Andrés Segovia come to play in the Assembly Hall. Mom sang with the Gilbert and Sullivan group in the Elting Room (and Town Hall) and that was great fun! Ted Scott, Robin Galt, Arthur Landers—wonderful singers!"

Carol Caspar Hayn (1960) has many wonderful memories of Exeter:

Nancy Bissell and Betsy Bickel (Photo courtesy of Nancy Bissell Goldcamp)

Crisp Fall days on the playing fields; everyone trooping across the bridge to the football stadium on Saturday afternoon. Student pranks—all the hymnals removed from the students' benches in the auditorium, so only the faculty on the stage were singing. Plays, with boys taking all the parts, female as well as male. The formality of dining hall meals with waiters serving the food. (How anachronistic that seems now!) Skating up the Exeter River and seeing these unbelievably long skate marks when around the bend came Principal Saltonstall, skating serenely and gracefully back to the starting point. Strong male voices joining in hymns at Philips Church. Not realizing until later what an un-typical upbringing I had!

Kathy Seabrooke Megathlin (1961) remembers:

going skating, attending wrestling matches and football games, going to the gym, the cage, plays and so forth. I recall the science building: I am very glad Mr. Mayo-Smith never found out I let all the mice out of the cages in his lab. The cannon balls from the town park were put into the toilets until the town permanently affixed them at the cannon sites. (Try to lift one out of a toilet!) Val Bosetto's Volkswagen was lifted onto the chapel stage. I know who did that one but do not know if it is still secret information.

What I really miss most are the wrestling meets in the pit. I can still smell the sweat and dampness of the cage. I can see my Dad, coach Ted Seabrooke, calmly on the edge of his chair with a roll of tape on his thumb, always encouraging and iterating the phrase, "Be smart." I was always there with my mother, sister, young brother and Frankie Irving for support.

How Their Experiences Affected Them

Incidents in the dorm, in the dining hall, and on the school campus had a lasting effect on how the daughters felt about themselves. When they were pre-teen, there was a feeling of fun and good times. Students were brothers, and life was good. When the girls became teenagers, things changed dramatically for most of them.

Edith Leonard Greene (1944) didn't feel that "the things the boys left in the dorm after they graduated helped my self-image. It looked like the cast-offs of the rich, like a Chinese junk ship. It just made me feel poor. The faculty were not paid much; we had to eat in the dining hall, we lived in a dorm apartment with nothing of our own to build on. What was there that was ours?"

Marilyn Easton (1958) reflects upon a variety of issues.

> When I was about twelve I went home with a town girl and her mother sent me packing. She told her daughter that I was different from them because I didn't have to work for a living the way they did.

> It felt like faculty were second class members of a wealthy family: the 'tutor' (teacher) in the family was 'staff,' and regarded as such by the upper class students.

> Students imported girls for the dances even if they were dating a local girl. That made the local girls, town or faculty daughter, feel unworthy, betrayed.

> Going to the dining hall was an ordeal. All conversation stopped when I entered. Then, when I sat down, it started up again. This situation contributed to a feeling of paranoia and shyness. I was always on display. The result was that I felt I had to watch myself doing something. I was "looking on," rather than being in the moment.

> Both my brother and I believe that we became psychologists partly because we never really belonged anywhere as children. As faculty we were not really Academy students as teens, even the boys. We weren't really part of the town as we were Academy people. As a result we were always observers of anything going on as well as partial participants. This isn't all that much fun in real life, but it is essential for a good therapist.

> Extreme rage at institutions which place the security of their own status quo, forms, rituals, routines over the feelings and needs of their members go directly back to being a faculty

brat. I've been tilting at the windmills of defective institutions my whole life. I always lose in the end, but I keep on doing it.

For Margie Weeks (1966) "the Academy relegated women to second-class status while I was growing up. This of course was not acknowledged because, by virtue of affiliation, either as wife or daughter, one could enjoy the benefits of first-class status, but it was the position of affiliation that stuck, and for some of us, it may have been defining."
Margaret Cox Abbot (1967) wrote:

> Well....there were 800 of them and only four faculty daughters my same age. WE WERE ICONS on campus.

> The years I grew up at Exeter, until I was fifteen and went away to school, have left a huge impression on me. I thought for years when I entered a room, any room, that all eyes were on me, because growing up as a young girl with 800 boys in a small town, all eyes *were* on me. I was the object of curiosity, rumors and pranks. But I loved being the center of attention, although many faculty daughters in the days of all boys, hated it and became quite shy. I went from an all-boys' school to an all-girls' school, so there was no middle ground. It wasn't until I got to college that I had a normal peer group.

A number of daughters felt they had to prove to the town students that they were not "stuck up" or "snobs." Margaret Cox Abbott found that "the 'townies,' however, considered Academy people to be 'superior,' above the rank and file. There was a veiled animosity."

Some had friends both in the town and at the Academy and felt there were no overtones because they were Academy. Another daughter was involved in the town because her father was a politician and knew everyone. She found it was hard at times in the public schools because of the real

Ethel Doe, with Emily Perry, Roma Leacock, and Judith Fiske
(Photo courtesy of Judith Fiske Gross)

town/gown divide. And another had an impression of being a second-class citizen because she was a girl, and at the same time and for the same reason, much sought after. She also developed an unreal picture of married life because her father was home for lunch, was as likely as her mother to be at home when she came in from school, and was around all summer.

Sarah Coffin O'Connor (1969) owes much to her family, who were profoundly committed to making sure she never heard "no" just because she was a girl. "I was encouraged to go to whatever academic institution I wanted, and to do whatever I wanted academically or professionally. But it remains in my head that the only educational opportunity where I *was* told 'no' just because of gender was at the Academy. That doesn't spoil the happy memories of an easy on-campus childhood, the wonderful friends I made who went to Exeter and the amount of activities Exeter provided to enrich my life because I was there as a faculty child."

Lydia Day Hart (1970) was the Principal's Daughter, a position which was almost as difficult as being the President's Daughter. Academy students came over to the house on Front Street as friends of her brother, or for some event hosted by her parents.

> Once the students found out I was the Principal's Daughter I became hands-off, much to my dismay and frustration, as I was not interested in any boy friend/girl friend relationships. Being a tom-boy, I just wanted friends.
>
> I have found it somewhat cathartic to write about a period of my life that was especially unhappy and be able to finally put it to rest. Thank you for the opportunity.

Maria Lynch Puro (1970) remembers:

> the sting I felt when walking across campus one day I heard a wolf whistle from an open window in Webster Hall. I felt exposed and humiliated mixed with a twinge of pleasure that I was being noticed. Most of the time, however, I preferred not to receive such attention. We lived on Elliot Street at this time and when I wanted to walk downtown I usually chose to walk the length of Elliot Street then turn up Front

Street rather than expose myself to unwanted attention by crossing campus.

I had a wonderful childhood and feel where I was had a lot to do with that. I was born in 1952 in a time when several faculty families had children, most of whom were boys. Becky Niebling, Susan Brownell and I were the girl core of this group. I loved all the opportunities for play. Lots of hide and seek in the Amen, Cilley and Wentworth quadrangle. Skating on the outdoor rink was a favorite. I rode my bike all around town and to school in good weather, and felt at home and safe as could be on campus. A little later there were lots of ball games at the flagpole, football and baseball mostly. It wasn't great to always be left field in baseball or center in football, but it was fun enough that I usually wanted to play.

Lisa Compton Bellocchio, (1971) who attended Concord Academy, felt her experiences at Exeter affected her in a variety of ways. She helped her mother with teas and dinners, learning how to set a table with polished silver, ironed tablecloths, etc. "I found later on in the work world that others don't necessarily have that experience. Also, because housing at PEA was a 'given,' I felt 'beholden' so put up with a lot. In addition, while there, one's family is financially 'poor' (low salary) but surrounded by superior facilities: library, gym, playing fields, tennis courts. The expectation after PEA is that one can get the same high cost benefits on a low income which does not happen."

How a daughter responded to living in a closed, residential community depended upon many factors. Her own individuality contributed to how she responded to the forces around her. The attitude of her parents toward the institution, the lack of privacy, the attentions of the Academy students and the tension between the town and the school all had their effect. Growing up is hard work no matter where you live, and being female in an all-male school made it all the more challenging.

Chapter 17

After Coeducation

With the arrival of female students on campus, the lives of the wives and daughters changed dramatically. The attention once centered on them was now diffused, shared with women faculty and female students. The teen years became more bearable for the daughters now that the boys had other girls to catch their attention. However, as faculty daughters became full-fledged members of the student body, there were difficult adjustments for the students and teachers alike.

Education

Beth Brownell (1971) was the first female to receive a Phillips Exeter diploma. Apparently the Academy was not quite ready for girls, as the male pronoun still applied to all graduates.

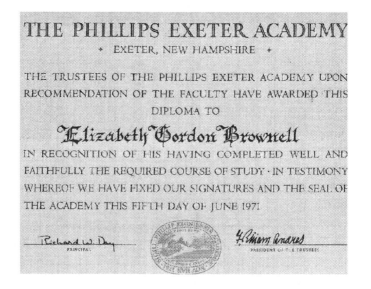

THE PHILLIPS EXETER ACADEMY

+ EXETER, NEW HAMPSHIRE +

THE TRUSTEES OF THE PHILLIPS EXETER ACADEMY UPON RECOMMENDATION OF THE FACULTY HAVE AWARDED THIS DIPLOMA TO

Elizabeth Gordon Brownell

IN RECOGNITION OF HIS HAVING COMPLETED WELL AND FAITHFULLY THE REQUIRED COURSE OF STUDY · IN TESTIMONY WHEREOF WE HAVE FIXED OUR SIGNATURES AND THE SEAL OF THE ACADEMY THIS FIFTH DAY OF JUNE 1971

The letter below illustrates a similar document given to Julia Lyford Lane, a member of the class of 1974, the fourth class to have women in the senior class. She did not even realize the Davis Fund and its award existed.

THE PHILLIPS EXETER ACADEMY
EXETER, NEW HAMPSHIRE
03833

December 20, 1973

Dear Julia:

The Davis Fund was established by Mr. George Davis in 1925 with the intent of providing a surprise gift for boys who have met their responsibilities at Exeter with enthusiasm and good will. It is a real pleasure for The Davis Fund Committee to present you with this token.

A pleasant and happy holiday.

Yours sincerely,

For the Committee
William B. Clark
Chairman

WBC/dn

(Courtesy of Julia Lyford Lane)

Julia continues her experiences with a description of being in the classroom.

As a female and a "fac brat" I was able to see and understand the foibles and fallibility of both the male faculty and students. I never felt in awe of them. I think this may have disturbed some of my teachers when I became an actual student. I don't remember ever actually consciously taking advantage of this position, but in retrospect I'm amused by its very existence and possible implications. As it was, I do suspect that many of the "old guard" were put off balance simply by the increasing presence of female energy and points of view.

Being part of the transformation was at once exciting and frustrating. Having inside knowledge of the "Emperor's underclothes" made the projected public image of the institution seem somewhat pretentious and also separated me, and other female fac brats, from the uninformed, uninitiated "new girls." It also made dating difficult for obvious reasons, as it was a two-way street with the sense that observers were everywhere. This is true for any faculty-child-as-student but we, as women, were under even more scrutiny.

Susie Cole Ross (1977) never felt fully accepted as a student at the Academy, because she *was* female.

I felt that many teachers and students thought we were unworthy of our places and damn lucky to be there. In my case, they may have been right, so I was determined to prove that I was as intelligent (or at least as studious) and as classy as any of my classmates. Nine of us comprised the first class of

Tootie and Susie Cole with Kathy and Dot Dunbar

(Photo courtesy of Dot Dunbar)

freshman girls and hence graduated as the first four-year-senior girls. I couldn't understand why every boy knew my name freshman year. I intentionally chose Connecticut College, previously a women's college, because it had a tradition of respecting the intellectual contributions of women. At PEA I learned that I could face any challenge; at Connecticut I learned that I had value and intellect.

Margaret Bravar Demopoulos (1983) attended the Academy while her mother was teaching in the Music Department. She realized the immersion of both students and faculty in school life and how much PEA demanded of them both, helping her to understand the pressures on her mother as a faculty member.

Cynthia Gutmann Morgan (1987) found that having a father who was an Academy math teacher was very helpful. Not only could he help her with homework, but he was also aware of the teaching styles of other teachers and could explain things to her in different ways.

Home

Cynthia Crowe (1976) felt she had the best of two worlds as a teen:

I took advantage of the social and cultural activities PEA offered, without having to follow the stringent rules the students followed. I also had the advantage of having my parents work close by so I could see them often. I met a lot of people I would never otherwise have met. Parents of PEA students included a Supreme Court Justice, film directors and cinematographers.

The disadvantages of living on campus were that the other faculty members all knew the faculty kids, which made it difficult to have any sort of anonymity. I also missed home-cooked, family meals with my own family. Overall, though, the good far outweighed the bad.

Julie Rindfleish Granville (1977) remembers and values her experience of growing up on campus:

One of the unique things about growing up at the Academy was having first-hand knowledge of my father's work life. Today, my girls jump at the chance to go to "Take

Your Daughter to Work Day," an annual opportunity to demystify their dad's daily trip into Manhattan. The concept is rather foreign to me; living at the Academy there was an absolute seamlessness between home and work. My father was in and out of our home apartment all day long. *He* was the one who wielded the thermometers and offered us shot glasses of coke when we were home sick. And if his class and sports schedule allowed it, we took afternoon trips to hike on the beach or get soft ice cream at the Weathervane.

Although I realize now that his job was 24/7, as they say, I never felt infringed upon because he was always *right there.* Yes, there were times when he shut the door to his study and cranked up the classical music so loud a bomb could have gone off and he wouldn't have heard it. But my memories by and large were of a dad who was always nearby. I could walk by his classroom window on a warm spring afternoon and hear his (rather loud) voice. I could sit next to him in the living room as he graded papers or joked with students as they checked in.

I was well aware that moral decisions were being made at faculty meetings, and learned that adults could disagree and still have respect—if not great affection—for one another. This "up close and personal" exposure to the adult world is rare for most children, and it enhanced the values I took away from childhood.

As I compare notes with friends who had "normal" childhoods I also recognize that what set life at the Academy apart was the tight-knit sense of community that is an inevitable by-product of boarding school life. From the simple experience of eating at dining hall together every night and sharing the same pathways and common places, everyone could not help but know everyone else—and I suppose the adults knew more about each other than we kids could even begin to imagine! We were families who not only lived and worked together, but also socialized together. I remember dressing up and passing hors d'oeuvres at many a cocktail or dinner party.

(As a kid, you learned how to be "sociable" whether you liked it or not.) Families at Exeter even shared holiday traditions. One of my all-time favorites was the caroling party at Christmastime. I do not recall a single Thanksgiving dinner when we didn't have someone "extra" at the table—an unmarried faculty member, an International student, or another family who, like us, lived far away from their grand-parents. And finally, it is hard to forget those rare but indelible moments of sudden tragedy which cannot help but bind a community together.

I am certain there were people—particularly some faculty wives—who must have found life at Exeter absolutely sti-fling. And whether you went to the Academy or Exeter High, being a faculty teenager in a place of total exposure was surely not easy. But to be a child in such an environment was, more often than not, wonderful.

Susie Cole Ross (1977) as a young child had a wonderful time play-ing all over the campus. "All campus was our playground, but it also meant that mothers knew what was going on and would call each other. I had been adopted by Marta Snow and Patty Heath as their only daughter as they both had all boys. When Daphne Moutis and I were little, we dressed in fluffy skirts, and did the Can-Can, flashing the stu-dents as they walked by the patio outside the Elting Room. We forgot that Mrs. Heath lived next door in Wheelwright Hall. The mothers came bustling up: Van was hot, and Mom had the ruler. We knew we had done the wrong thing. It turned out that Patty had called Van and Tootie and alerted them to the 'goings-on.'"

Entertainment

Ice skating continued to be a favorite. Skating on the river had to wait for the sanction of Susie Cole Ross' grandfather, Phil Wilson, the hockey coach, and Henry Bragdon who tested the ice on the river and declared when it was safe: Susie remembers how they helped with tending the rink.

The four grandchildren would often help the students shovel the rink before games behind his home on Marston Lane. I remember helping Gramma make hot cocoa and passing it out to the team after shoveling." Susie's mother, Tootie, remembers her mother, Sue Wilson, bringing out a kitchen stool and blankets to keep warm to watch games while skaters used the boiler house to get warm.

Hockey at Marston Lane rink c. 1954
(Courtesy of Academy Archives)

Susie's parents often had students in for birthday parties.

I remember when I was about five flinging myself on the kitchen floor in despair because I knew my birthday was upcoming (I did not realize that it was still a month away), and yet my mother told me that the telltale angel food cake resting upside down on top of the refrigerator, the cake over which I had been salivating, was not for me. In fact, it was not for anyone in the family. It was for one of dad's advisees whose mother can't be here to make him a cake, and I would not even get a bite of it. Needless to say I made my frustration and consternation known.

Stories

The daughters have a wealth of stories to tell of family life and their lives as students.

When Susie Cole Ross (1977) was small, she knew she was strictly forbidden to make noise near her dad's classroom during the day, much less to go over there.

One day I fell and badly scraped my knee. I ran home to mom in tears, but she wasn't there. More frustrated than frightened, I ran around the quad looking for her. Then I heard my dad's voice from his open classroom window. I checked my knee and hoped that there was enough blood to make it dramatic, to excuse my interrupting his class. I walked up the huge marble stairs and into a cavernous marble foyer. Dad's door was three times my height, awesome, dark mahogany. My tiny fisted knock rang out through the echoing edifice. Before I could run away, Dad opened the door, smiled at my frightened face, and bent down to swoop me up, grabbed a sugar cube from the bowl (his office doubled as the history faculty room in those days) and held me on his lap without missing a beat of his lecture on ancient roman architecture. I still love sugar cubes and my comfy place in the austere Academy.

Freshman year I remember coming out of the Academy Building with my first boyfriend. So in love. For two weeks. All of a sudden, behind me, I hear, "Ahem, what is going on???" I saw Mr. Kurtz grab Dad's sleeve saying, "Nothing that ain't been going on for years, Don."

I had thirteen brothers, my father's advisees. My dolls got decapitated, and I was teased about curling my hair. The boys got their comeuppance when I became coxswain for the crew team. Then I got to tell boys twice my weight what to do all day long. Because the Academy still felt like an all-boys' school, I was constantly competing with boys. As the only girl traveling with the team to other boys' schools, there would be no locker room for me. Always the odd person out.

I remember Dad coming into my room to ask my permission to become Dean of the Academy the summer before my lower year. He thought it would affect my status and how much time he had for me. He was right—for better and for worse. But I have a fond memory of racing him (wearing an austere suit) home from Jeremiah Smith Hall and yelling over my shoulder to him, "Administrators can't run!" much to the surprise of several students who had not seen his playful side.

I remember how Dad kept slippers next to the bed so that he could step right into them. Once a boy dropped a chair on the top floor and when dad got to the top of the stairs another boy clicked a stopwatch and said, "Not bad, Mr. Cole. 13 point 9 seconds!

Cynthia Gutmann Morgan (1987) recalls an amusing incident illustrating what can happen when your parent is a teacher and you are a student. "One day during my senior year I was walking with three or four friends about twenty feet behind my father. In an attempt to get his attention I called out, 'Daddy' several times. He did not respond, so I yelled, 'Mr. Gutmann.' This got his attention. My friends had also not noticed my previous attempts, and asked, surprised, 'You call your father Mr. Gutmann?!'"

How Living at the Academy Affected Daughters

Julia Lyford Lane (1974) valued her Exeter experience "because it provided truly unique challenges to my individuality and caused me to justify and value who I am and what I believe. This did not necessarily manifest while I was actually there, but I believe that I was fundamentally strengthened by being at that place at that time."

Susie Cole Ross (1977) spoke of the feelings generated by being a scholarship student:

All faculty children were on scholarship and therefore worked at scholarship jobs, along with the boarding students. Since only scholarship students worked at the school, I was associated with that status of student.

I also had well-to-do but needy friends who missed home and followed me to my refrigerator, soft cats and sensible, accessible mother whenever possible. I always knew I had something more valuable than all their money. I recall being a bit self-conscious about my clothes, most of which I made, but I was also proud of my skill.

How did Exeter impact my life? I am terribly competitive with men and many of my friends are men. PEA lead me to my career: With my learning disability (dyslexia), I was more interested in people than books. And I found out I was able to compete intellectually at the Academy. I found college easy by comparison. So I guess that's why I've gone from working with kids with disabilities to kids at an Academy (Loomis Chaffee) who are very bright. I always knew there are no dumb kids at that school, just that their resources have not been tapped. At PEA, people believed I could do it. My work is my calling. It is like I get to heal old wounds.

Kate Rindfleisch McGrath (1981) shared her feelings:

I was conscious of being a bit less advantaged in terms of money, knowledge of New York City, these kinds of things. More a product of being from New Hampshire than of being a faculty kid. How I was perceived by town students was most felt in junior high. I felt that my status was high as an Academy daughter. Socially, nothing changed if people knew, but I noticed that it was less of a triumph for me to get good grades, for example, since perhaps I was a faculty kid. I did feel very proud of my Dad for having a job at PEA. This gave me a kind of confidence. I am also proud that my Mom was so involved in Exeter life, both the town and the school, and seemed to be so happy and have so many friends."

For Wendy Crowe Watson (1983) "growing up in that environment with the excellent facilities and programs and students as role models gave me the opportunities, courage and support to try out many different sports and instilled a value for education that I now realize. Looking back, I realize I felt very 'safe' there—both physically in the environment and emotionally with my family and "student family" and other faculty families such as the Mahoneys and Dennehys."

Conclusions

The daughters of faculty viewed the school from a different vantage point than their mothers. As young children, the daughters' lives were without responsibility, full of fun, antics and mischief. Before the school became coeducational, however, their experiences as they grew into their teen years were not always happy ones. They were the few young women among many young men. The stares in the dining hall, the unwelcome attention, and the lack of privacy in some of the apartments were their primary discomforts.

After 1970, coeducation dramatically changed the experience of the faculty daughters. They were no longer the only teen girls on campus, and could enter the dining hall or walk the paths without feeling all eyes on them. If daughters were set apart it was more because they were children of faculty and less because they were female.

The daughters who were among the first female students had the hardest roles to play—those of first female students and faculty daughters as well. All in all, after the Academy became coeducational the experiences of the daughters were more affirming than before.

Life at a boarding school is very like life elsewhere, reflecting the general culture, however, it has its own character. The defining difference between life on the "inside" and life on the "outside" is the compression of feelings, events and attention—the knowledge that the immediate world "is watching." For those who live on campus, surrounded by the students and by the institution, this defines their world. How they respond to this atmosphere depends on a host of factors—timing in one's life, world events outside that change everyone and everything, and who we are to begin with. By examining this world, we can begin to better understand in what ways this life affected who we became.

APPENDIX

Oral History Project
Women of Exeter: The Faculty Spouse
Barbara Eggers
Instructor, Department of History
May 1988
"Committee to Enhance the Status of Women" Newsletter May 1988

Over the past year, I've had the opportunity to talk with the wives of emeriti about their years at the Academy. While I was struck by how the lives of these women parallel the changes of our society during the past 40 years, the difference in expectations over the generations was quite apparent. Most women saw their roles as part of their husband's and found great gratification in that role. In the '40s and '50s most women defined their lives' expectations (or career) as "home and family." Today a women's definition would be larger, including goals and aspirations outside the home.

Women have been an unrecorded part of the school since Elizabeth Phillips signed the original deed of gift with her husband, John, in 1781 and gave up her "dower rights" to the land. About a year ago, Ed Desrochers, (Academy Archivist) and Jackie Thomas (Academy Librarian), suggested an oral history project about women at Exeter prior to co-education. The objective of the oral history project is to capture the experiences and recollections of those women who served the Academy as faculty wives and as staff members over the last several decades. Further, this project would also help us know the Academy better and understand some of its changes over time. Being interested in the historical aspect of the school, I agreed to help. With support from the Day Fund, we began the project during the summer of 1987.

Initially, we identified 26 emeriti wives whose time at Exeter spanned a couple of decades and who might be interested in the project. Twenty-one women responded to our initial inquiry, and of the 14 who agreed to be interviewed, I interviewed 10 last August.

We were interested in knowing what these women did at Exeter, how they perceived their roles, and in general what their life was like. While the results of any survey like this will be highly impressionistic, the sense these women left me with was very positive. With few exceptions, these women enjoyed their life at Exeter, and felt fortunate to have been a part of the school. The sample, however, was somewhat self-selecting and perhaps predictable in its results. All of their husbands were faculty members for 30 to 40 years, with the earliest coming to the school in 1917, and all were life-long marriages.

Apart from the presence of female faculty and male spouses, the biggest contrast to today is quite noticeably the two-career family. According to Historical Statistics, in 1983, 52.9% of women worked compared to 31.4% in 1950, and 24.8% in 1930. Today the vast majority of faculty spouses work outside the home, whether at an actual paying job, continued schooling, or political and civic action groups.

Few of the women surveyed attempted careers outside the home, in spite of the fact that all had post-high school education. But none objected; they never felt they had given up anything. Most of the women had attended colleges such as Radcliffe (6), Smith, Vassar, or Mt. Holyoke, and majored in various disciplines (chemistry, social work, counseling, economics, theatre). While some took part-time or short-term jobs at different points during their marriages, only two women used their specific college preparation in employment while at Exeter. More significantly, all women volunteered their time with various organizations in town, most notably with the public school system and including elected positions with the School Board, through their volunteer efforts, the faculty wives founded the Exeter Day School and were responsible for the installation of the blinking light at the crosswalk on Front Street.

Most of the women noted that there were no stated or official expectations of the faculty wife for any specific Academy functions, yet certainly the unwritten assumption was there. At the same time, however, the women saw these tasks as part of their role as wives. One woman wrote that the high point of her time at Exeter was "helping in the dorm with my husband." Another woman had scrapbooks and mementos of her dorm years of the same care and quality devoted to family keepsakes. The "close partnership for a husband and wife and participation of our children in that life" was the way one wife recalled her Academy years. The theme of teamwork and partnership played over and over again during the interviews.

Wives were quite willing to help with their husbands' jobs but drew the line as what that help included. The women would routinely check in students when a husband was at a meeting or supervising evening study halls. Wives also ran the dorm for an entire weekend if the husband had to be out of town. To have another male faculty come in would have been improper with the wife and children at home alone. They also helped with small but necessary things—the use of an iron, a button replaced in an emergency, the use of a phone—services not too different from those performed rather routinely today by faculty spouses. But one school program that did meet opposition from the wives, and was subsequently curtailed, was the request that they serve juice to the students in the infirmary. Volunteers were not readily forthcoming, and some women stated their objection to the program as being well beyond reasonable expectations.

In a social capacity and as support for their husbands, faculty wives helped to serve tea to students or distinguished guests, chaperoned Saturday night dances and movies (considered faculty duty), cooked hamburgers after the movies, gave birthday parties in their apartments for advisees and close friends, cooked occasional Sunday breakfasts or held open house on Sunday afternoon, and "watched 3,000 athletic events."

During the single sex days of the Academy faculty wives were very important to the theatre—from dressing boys for female parts to female make-up to acting the female roles themselves. And several women stated their enjoyment in these professional tasks. A faculty wife trained in theatre once taught an over subscribed theatre course and remarked that that was the "best time I had as a faculty wife." Faculty wives also used their training or special talents to tutor boys, particularly in English and languages.

Most wives found few drawbacks associated with living at the Academy, but most universally those were related to family life—the "difficulty of raising children in the 3rd floor apartment." One women, who came to the Academy during the mid-1950's, described her 4th-floor residence. It consisted of "a living room, bathroom, and bedroom. The refrigerator was in the hall landing, the hot plate in the bathroom, and we washed dishes in the bathtub." By the time her first child was born, the apartment had a kitchen, "but the baby slept in the bath-room."

One common theme was the lack of privacy or the lack of family time. Most women recalled that there was technically no time when one was "off-duty." Until 1969, children under the age of 6 were not allowed in the dining hall, thus arrangements for a baby-sitter had to be made so the wife could have dinner with her husband in the dining hall. Most women had a girl from the town come in to feed the children, or perhaps fed the children early, then had someone to watch them while the parents went to dinner.

Occasional flashbacks of frustration or disappointment also entered our discussions. One women told of her excitement about coming to Exeter as a young wife, but during her first year in the dorm, that initial excitement turned into serious doubt about her decision. Sensing her frustration, and with the best of intentions, the husband arranged a "get-away" weekend in New York City. Saturday, as the curtain went up for Act I of a new hit play, *Tea and Sympathy* (Robert Anderson'35), it seemed as though Exeter was everywhere! The set design bore an obvious resemblance to Williams House, and of course the story involved a young wife who was definitely unsuited to her role as a Master's wife. The woman laughed when she recalled the irony of her "escape," and her return to Exeter for over 30 years.

When women did show signs of bitterness, however faint, it always involved a concern for fairness for their faculty husband. Perhaps a "choice" apartment had been granted to someone "out of turn." Or perhaps the reward for a job "well done" in the dormitory was more years in the dorm. Perhaps someone was considered "too valuable" to leave the dorm while some other faculty member, indifferent to his role in the dorm, was allowed to move out—"for the sake of the dorm."

With both family and school responsibilities, these women led very full lives and, from listening to them talk, apparently satisfying lives. While there were some limitations on family life, the social and cultural opportunities to get together with friends, meet famous artists and musicians, hear renowned guest lecturers, and live in a close community in that partnership with their husbands seemed to fulfill their expectations. And in doing so they gave a great deal of themselves to the Academy.

Has the role of the Academy spouse changed? One woman lamented the "loss of faculty wives to the dorm because of their going to work." Yet it seems a lot of those unofficial services are still provided by that working spouse. Conversations with faculty families often reveal quite unintentionally the joint dorm activities. He or she bakes cookies, drives to "grill," unlocks doors, fixes computers, helps install rugs, starts the fire for the picnic, collects the broken-down bike in Hampton and any other needed tasks. Today's dorm faculty would still lament the loss of privacy and family time, yet most of us do have kitchens and don't do dishes in the bathtub. All family members have use of the dining hall, regardless of age. And the recent opening of the Academy Day Care Center indicates the Academy's response to today's changed situation of the two-career family.

Did the women I interviewed wish they had today's opportunities? Most were very glad for coeducation at Exeter and happy that women now had more choices open to them. Some felt that the time demanded of a job took necessary time from the family. But to these emeriti wives, the key word was "choice." They had made their choices of marriage and family, and by extension, their choices included their contributions to Exeter.

Peg Aaronian's Thursday Meditation

Ten years after the Academy became coeducational, Peg Aaronian (1971), faculty wife and instructor at the University of New Hampshire, felt that many students were not aware of the qualities possessed by the faculty wives outside of their role as "faculty wife." Her meditation challenges the students to see the wives in a new light. Excerpts from her talk and the Quiz she handed out follow:

Excerpts from
Peg Aaronian's Thursday Meditation

17 April 1980

I tried to explain to my writing class at UNH about the condition of being a "faculty spouse" at Exeter,...that the affliction was formerly called being a "faculty wife" since it plagued women only, but that certain changes over the last decade has allowed the spread of this condition to men as well. [Coeducation instituted in 1970.]

In many of the women I know, the ailment has caused a considerable portion of their identity to disappear. All—that is—but the Exeter aspects. The aspects of a spouse's life at Exeter usually include living in a dorm, eating in a dining hall, unlocking student doors, signing out-of-towns when faculty members are unavailable and taking messages from the janitors and the deans. To many in the Exeter community— adults and adolescents—spouses are one-dimensional.

When the school minister, David McIheney, asked me to speak at the Thursday Meditation, an Exeter graduate in my writing class encouraged me to talk about faculty wives. She told me how much she had learned about wives at Exeter at a Mother's Day seminar that some of us participated in a couple of years ago.

"I couldn't believe it when a faculty wife, Caren Schubart, explained what she did at work," the student said. "It was so exciting to see what everyone did. When I was at Exeter I didn't know anything about them. I didn't even know Merryn Spurrier, another faculty wife, had a husband."

Ahh. An invisible husband.

She suddenly became aware of an aspect of her school she never knew about...maybe because she was pleased to see so many of her own gender married, with children and a career but still part of her school.

I believe the complaint about being invisible comes when one is afflicted with "faculty-spouse-itis" because we have come to assign that label to anyone who is "married to the person who teaches at PEA." We define in terms of the institution when the person being described may have only the most tenuous link with the institution by being married to part of it. And when we define in terms of an institution, we see that person only in the institutional environment. Their skills and talents are hardly ever uncovered, let alone tapped.

You cannot use something unless you know it is available. I'm sure many of us would be happy to have our expertise used—by students and teachers. But there's a world of difference between being asked to speak to a class and being asked to bake a cake for it.

Don't feel you have to delve into the lives of all the spouses on campus. Just stop...look...and listen. In my quick, unscientific survey of spouses, I found a tremendous range of interest, talents, and jobs. About 15% of us work right here...in the music and art departments, in the infirmary, library, student center and in Jeremiah Smith.

In our ranks we have expertise in needlework, dance, drama, in colonial restoration. Faculty spouses have long supplied woman power to Exeter's public and private schools, to the Democratic and Republican Parties, to the League of Women Voters, to the Exeter Hospital, Child and Family

Services, Visiting Nurses, Family Planning and more recently, the anti-nuclear movement.

Faculty spouses have worked as executive secretaries, as translators and interpreters, and in the Peace Corps. Some are bi-or multi-lingual. Among the spouses we have a recreation department basketball coach, a librarian who travels to Rhode Island every other week for library science courses. Some twenty-five percent of us work at home most of the time including our only househusband. We have doctoral and bachelor's degree candidates. We have people trained in chemistry, city planning, math, French, English literature, physical education and history to name but a few.

Now let me ask you something—as I read my list did you attach names and faces to those descriptions? If you can't, your education about Exeter is incomplete.

I think it's important that you know that the person with a Ph.D. in Slavic Literature is the same person who bakes cookies for you…and is the same person otherwise known by the anonymous label of faculty spouse.

Quiz

1. Name 7 spouses who are self-employed or who own their own businesses.
2. Name 5 spouses who work in libraries. Extra credit if you can identify the library.
3. Name 2 spouses who commute daily to Massachusetts.
4. Name 3 who work in areas related to medicine/health care.
5. Many spouses work in education. Identify the following:
   At Exeter High School (3)
   At Exeter Junior High (2)
   At the Exeter Elementary School (1)
   At the Greenland School (1)
   At a private school as a kindergarten teacher (1)
6. Four spouses teach at two universities. Identify each instructor, her field and university.

7. Within the last year five spouses have earned a Ph.D. or been in a doctoral program. Extra credit for correctly identifying each field of study.

8. Name two spouses who hold or have held elective office.

9. Who is the father-spouse?

10. Who is the full-time student?

11. Two spouses work in special education/child development fields. Identify.

12. Who sells real estate?

13. Who had been instrumental in organizing a hospice?

14. Name 13 spouses who work at PEA. Include only one name from the Summer School staff.

Wives who participated in the history

Numbers in parenthesis are the years they lived at the school.
Number of wives approached: 79 ; number who responded: 49

Libby Bickel (1936-1972)
Betty Brinckerhoff (1947-1965)
Connie Brown (1962-1997)
Shirley Brownell (1958-1988)
Judy Buechner (1958-1967)
Barbara Burgin (1964-1972)
Judy Casey (1969-1971)
Helen Clark (1937-1976)
Rosemary Coffin (1953-1987)
Elizabeth Compton(1955-1985)
Susan (Tootie) Cole(1947-1988)
Barbara Crowe (1968-1994)
Andrea Deardorff (1962-1993)
Dorothy Dunbar (1955-1993)
Mary Echols (1957-1981)
Frances Ekstrom (1969-1999)
    Currently faculty
Margo Fish (1961-1964)
Mary Fleischman (1956-1967)
Margery Forbes (1962-1987)
Anne Gleason (1967-1971)
Lois Gutmann (1963-1999)
Carol Hamblet (1979-1989)
Corinna Hammond (1973-1999)
Patty Heath (1947-1989)
Nancy Heyl (1947-1975)
Frances Irving (1946-1988)
Barbara James (1972-2000)
Doris Leighton (1934-1971)
Barbara Little (1939-1948)
Joan Lyford (1963-1986)
Charlotte Manning (1963-1966)
Katharyn Saltonstall Moore (1932-1963)
Joyce Morgan (1969-1995)

Van Moutis (1955-1978)
Libby Niebling (1941-1974)
Nancy Pierce (1971-1978)
Carol Rindfleisch (1968-1990)
Anne Rogers (1967-1973)
Jeanne Kurtz Smeeth (1974-1984) .
Marta Snow (1959-1985)
Mary Stevens (1942-1970)
Sarah Guffy Stone (1965-1969)
Madeline Stuckey (1971-1983)
Marcia Taft (1951-1989)
Betty Terry (1967-1997)
Jackie Thomas (1957-1996 and the present)
Margo Trout (1961-1968)
Carol Tucker (1980-1989)
Jean Walker (1963-1990)

From Archival Material:

Violette Bennett (1929-1965)
Amanda Cilley (1864-1899)
Emily Perry Cox (1948-1970)
Betty Caspar (1950-1974)
Harriette Easton (1932-1971)
Mabel Fiske (1920-1938)
Louise Funkhouser (1932-1966)
Rebecca Hogg (1931-1961)
LaRu Lynch (1939-1984)
Lilja Rogers (1923-1966)
Ellen Scott (1932-1967)
Helen Stuckey (1917-1954)
Lucy Weeks (1935-1972)
Susan Wilson (1942-1966)

Questionnaire sent to Wives

Where did you go to high school?

When did you graduate?

If you went to college, where did you go?

When did you graduate?

Indicate further education or other category of education.

Did you work before coming to Exeter? What kind of work did you do?

When did you arrive on campus? Month and year.

When did you leave or retire?

What was your state of mind when you first arrived on campus? Did you feel mature, immature, naive, or surprised by what you discovered boarding school life was like?

How long had you been married when you arrived on campus?

Where did you live before coming to Exeter?

If you lived or worked at a boarding school before coming to Exeter, how did it affect your anticipation of the job at Exeter?

Was Exeter different than the boarding school where you had been?

If you didn't know anything about boarding schools, how did that affect your anticipation?

In which dormitories did you live at PEA?

Did your husband encourage you to be active in the dormitory? Did you hand out the master key or sign permission slips?

What was your relationship with him vis-à-vis the school: "I am here to support him in what he does" or "PEA is his job, I have my own" or a combination?

Did you entertain the students in your home? In what ways?

Did the school pay you for these activities and if so, how much?

Did you attend student functions such as dances, plays, concerts? Were you asked to chaperone?

Did you act in plays, make costumes, play in orchestra, etc.?

Did the school ask you to entertain for specific events such as teas or coffees for the parents or the Trustees?

At what age were your children allowed to eat in the dining hall? What did you do if they did not come with you?

Was there a school policy about wives working either on or off campus? Did that affect you personally?

Did you work outside the home? In what capacity?

What community activities such as AAUW, LWV, Red Cross, Exeter Players, or Hospital did you engage in? Did you do volunteer work? Where?

What was the national climate at the time you were at the school?

Were you aware of discrepancies between life at the school and the national climate at the time? Were you aware later?

Before 1970, your daughter could not attend the academy. Where did she go to school? When did she graduate?

Did the school help out with tuition for another boarding school? If so, what percent of the tuition did they offer?

After 1970, when your daughter could attend Exeter, did she choose to?

What year did she graduate?

If she chose not to attend Exeter, where did she go and when did she graduate?

We would like to contact faculty daughters with questionnaires of their own. It would be helpful if you entered your daughter's names and address here. (We would like all their names, but questionnaires will be sent only to those who have graduated from high school.)

I understand that the information I share may be used in *Wives and Daughters Remember*.

Signature and date.

A Story of Your Own

This space is provided for you to write down memories of events you would like to share. Whether offered in a few sentences or several pages, your memories are the heart of *Wives and Daughters Remember*.

Daughters who participated in the history

Number is date of Graduation from high school.
Number of daughters approached: 85; responded: 45

Ann	Barry Lovering 1955	Judith	Fiske Gross 1942
Betsy	Bickel Hersam 1960	Cynthia	Gutmann Morgan 1987
Margaret	Bravar Demopoulos 1983	Margaret	Hogg Upham 1944
Ann	Brinckerhoff Mingledorff 1966	Lucy	Hulburd Richardson 1938
		Edith	Leonard Greene 1944
Ann	Broderick 1974	Anne	Leonard Whitney 1947
Martha	Brownell Grant 1973	Jane	Leonard 1950
Susan	Brownell Hodgson 1970	Dorothy	Lloyd Tyack 1947
Jennifer	Burgin Cogliano 1982	Julia	Lyford Lane 1974
Carol	Caspar Hayn 1960	Maria	Lynch Puro 1970
Ellen	Clark Peck 1961	Betsy	Macomber Ensor 1955
Margaret	Clarkson Schoene 1953	Judith	Macomber Morse 1957
Sarah	Coffin O'Connor 1969	Daphne	Moutis 1976
Susan	Cole Ross 1977	Emily	Perry Cox 1942
Lisa	Compton Bellocchio 1971	Eleonore	Phillips Sanderson 1952
Margaret	Cox Abbott 1967	Julie	Rindfleisch Granville 1977
Cynthia	Crowe 1976	Katie	Rindfleisch McGrath 1981
Wendy	Crowe Watson 1983	Elizabeth	Rhoades Aykroyd 1962
Charlotte	Cushwa Clark 1938	Joey	Saltonstall Dubois 1951
Lydia	Day Hart 1970	Kathy	Seabrooke Megathlin 1961
Jennifer	Deardorff Gardner 1985	Lucy	Weeks Peck 1957
Marilyn	Easton 1958	Margie	Weeks 1966
Jean	Finch Topping 1952	Marion	Wilson Chandler 1949
		Tootie	Wilson Cole 1946

Questionnaire sent to Daughters

What years did your family live at the academy?

Where did you go to high school?

When did you graduate?

When and how did you interact with Exeter students?

Did you have academy boys as friends?

Did you date academy students during your teen years?

Was your teacher-parent available for you or was he/she busy with students and advisees?

Before coeducation, daughters could not attend PEA. If you were unable to attend, what were your thoughts at the time? Now?

In which dormitories did you live?

Did your dormitory apartment have a private entrance?

Did your dormitory apartment feel like home?

In the dormitory apartment, was privacy an issue? Examples.

Did your dormitory apartment have a yard you felt was *yours*?

If you were not allowed to go to the dining hall, what did you do for meals when your parents went?

Did your family give birthday parties for the students? Did they have students in Saturday night? Did the dorm have a picnic at the end of the year? Did you join the students for these events?

Did you attend sports events, concerts, plays and lectures on campus? Which ones?

Did you go to the Saturday night movies in the gymnasium or assembly hall? Did you go ice skating at the school rinks?

What is your impression of how your parents felt about the school?

If you went to the academy, did you feel accepted as an equal by the other students and by the faculty, or was your status as faculty child as issue?

What was your involvement with the town? Did you, for instance, volunteer at the hospital, act in plays, attend town events, etc.?

How did you feel you were perceived by the town people in your status as academy daughter? Did you feel accepted by the town students and adults?

I understand that the information I share may be used in *Wives and Daughters Remember.*

Signature and date.

A Story Of Your Own

This space is provided for you to write down memories or events you would like to share. Whether offered in a few sentences or several pages, your memories are the heart of *Wives and Daughters Remember.*

Faculty Wives as Honorary Members of PEA Classes

Helen Clark	1945
Louise Clements	1931
Dorothy Dunbar	1945
Andi Grey	1971
Janet Gillespie Grindley	1929
Patricia Heath	1970
Barbara James	1974, 1985, 1993
Barbara Little	1945
Katharyn Saltonstall Moore	1924, 1950, 1963
Elizabeth Niebling	1934
Snookie Mangan Revay	1962
Lilja Rogers	1931, 1932
Jeanne G. Kurtz Smeeth	1949
Marta Snow	1965
Mary Stevens	1962
Helen Stuckey	1922, 1930
Jacquelyn Thomas	1969
Marcia Tingley	1948, 1964, 2001
Eleanor Tremallo	1970

Colleges and Universities attended by wives who responded to questionnaire

Antioch College: Masters in Education Organization and Management
Art School, not named
Boston College Graduate School of Social Work (Clinical)
Boston University : Masters in Sacred Music; Ph.D. in Classics
Brown University
Carnegie Mellon
College of St. Elizabeth
Cortland State Teachers College
Edinburgh University
Gettysburg College
Harvard College: Master of Arts in Teaching
Hospital Dietetics Masters program
Hunter College: Master of Arts in Art Education
Keene State
Lesley College
Manhattan College of the Sacred Heart
Massachusetts Institute of Technology
McGill University
Michigan State University
Mt. Holyoke College: BA (2); Masters of Arts
New York University Graduate School of Science
Notre Dame College: Masters in Education (2)
Ohio University
Ohio Wesleyan University
Pembroke
Pennsylvania State University
Radcliffe College (4)
Rhode Island School of Design
Sarah Lawrence
Simmons College

Smith College: BA (4); Masters of Science
Sorbonne
Stephens College
Swarthmore College (2)
T.C.U.
Teachers College, Columbus University: Masters in Economic Geography
Union Theological Seminary: Masters
University of Alabama: Masters of Arts
University of California, Santa Barbara
University of Kansas
University of Maryland
University of Maryland: Master of Arts
University of Massachusetts: Masters of Fine Arts in Painting
University of Michigan
University of New Brunswick
University of New Hampshire: BA (3); CAGS; Master of Arts in Teaching; Masters of Education (2)
University of North Carolina
University of Rochester
University of Southern Maine
Valparaiso University
Vassar College
Washington University
Wellesley College
Wells College (2)
Wheaton College
Wheelock College
Whittenburg College
William and Mary
Yale University: Ph.D. Slavic Languages and Literature

BIBLIOGRAPHY

Bell, Charles H., <u>A Historical Sketch of Phillips Exeter Academy</u>, Exeter, New Hampshire, Wm. B. Morrill, Printer. News-Letter Press 1883.

Cilley, Bradford, <u>Diary</u>, Phillips Exeter Academy Archives.

Coffin, Rosemary, <u>The Garland of Philippa</u>, Publishing Works, Exeter, New Hampshire ©2001.

Crosbie, Laurence M., <u>The Phillips Exeter Academy, A History</u>, The Plimpton Press, Norwood MA, ©1924.

Cunningham, H. Frank, <u>Familiar Sketches of the Phillips Exeter Academy</u>, James R. Osgood and Co. ©1883.

Easton, Marilyn, <u>Passionate Spinster: The Diary of Patty Rogers: 1785</u>, Xlibris ©2001 Marilyn J. Easton, Ph.D.

Echols, Edward C., editor, <u>The Phillips Exeter Academy, A Pictorial History</u>, Exeter Academy Press ©1970.

————.*Exonian, The*, weekly newspaper, Phillips Exeter Academy, Academy Archives.

Fiske, Mabel Cilley, <u>Memories of Family and Home in Exeter</u>, ©1967, copy in Phillips Exeter Academy Archives.

————.*Grapevine, The*, quarterly publication of Phillips Exeter Academy women, 1965-1977, Academy Archives.

<u>Life at Phillips Exeter</u>, Published by The Phillips Exeter Academy, Exeter, New Hampshire, 1913.

Phillips Exeter Academy Catalog, 1912-1913

Phillips Exeter Academy Catalog, 1895, Supplement. Exeter Historical Society 3373.7 Phillips Exeter Catalogue.

Rindfleisch, Norval, Standing Lessons, Writer's Showcase, New York, ©2002.

Saltonstall, William Gurden, John Phillips (1719-1795). Address to the Newcomian Club, 1951.

Street, Rev. George E., Historical Sketch of Dr. John Phillips, June 16, 1895. PEA Archives.

Williams, Myron R. The Story of Phillips Exeter, 1781-1956, Phillips Exeter Academy, Exeter NH ©1957.